Praise for *Dropping the Struggle*

"Surrender is an essential goal of all spiritual work. Letting go of the control that we never really had is both our great task and the key to a life of joy and inner peace. In *Dropping the Struggle*, Roger Housden has written a simple but brilliant guidebook to help us do just that. With inspiring poetry, engaging stories, and deep insight, this book is a heartful invitation to let go of fighting with life and open to the wisdom and love right inside us. I highly recommend this beautiful book!"

— JAMES BARAZ, author of *Awakening Joy* and cofounding teacher at Spirit Rock Meditation Center

"This wonderful book is an antidote to overachievement, a welcome respite from striving to 'have it all,' a voice of sanity in a world addicted to self-improvement. Irreverent, profound, and hard-hitting. I loved it."

— MARK MATOUSEK, author of *Ethical Wisdom*

"*Dropping the Struggle* is a beautifully written message from the heart that speaks directly to what my life needs now. An inspiring, life-changing book that challenges us to open our arms to the life we have rather than wishing we had something else."

— MARCI SHIMOFF, author of *Happy for No Reason*

"Gently and wisely, Roger Housden points to the timeless knowing within us, which dissolves the need to struggle with life, with others, and with ourselves."

— ROGER WALSH, MD, PHD, author of *Essential Spirituality*

"This book came to me just when I needed it, helping me to loosen my tight fist on how I want things to be and take another step toward acceptance. *Dropping the Struggle* is filled with rich inspiration from many sources, such as the great poet Rainer Maria Rilke, who tells us to 'Want the change. / Be inspired by the flame / Where everything shines as it disappears.' Thank you, Roger Housden, for giving us the old truths in a new way."

— ELLEN BASS, author of *Like a Beggar* and coauthor of
The Courage to Heal

"This book is a deep drink of water for my soul, which has run itself ragged with my own little self-improvement obstacle course. I read it because I trust Roger Housden. And I trust Roger Housden because he speaks the language of the heart: poetry. With luminous clarity, radical authenticity, and tender appreciation of the human predicament, *Dropping the Struggle* is more than a teaching and bigger than a book: it is an invitation to transform."

— MIRABAI STARR, translator of *Dark Night of the Soul*
and author of *Caravan of No Despair*

"Roger Housden's *Dropping the Struggle* is a book of confessions, advice, and easy-to-digest wisdom on how to lean into surrender and *beingness* in spite of our Western hardwiring of constant *doingness*. If you are seeking a path to the Sea of Tranquility, let this book be your guide."

— ARIELLE FORD, author of *Turn Your Mate into Your Soulmate*

"*Dropping the Struggle* is a wise, compassionate, fierce gift and gentle guide for living fully with more ease. Blending poetry, storytelling, and science, it leads the way toward a more open heart and mind."

— MARC LESSER, author of *Less* and
Know Yourself, Forget Yourself

DROPPING THE STRUGGLE

Other Books by Roger Housden

Travels through Sacred India

Sacred America: The Emerging Spirit of the People

Ten Poems to Change Your Life

Chasing Rumi: A Fable about Finding the Heart's True Desire

Ten Poems to Set You Free

Seven Sins for a Life Worth Living

Ten Poems to Last a Lifetime

Ten Poems to Open Your Heart

Risking Everything: 110 Poems of Love and Redemption

Dancing with Joy: 99 Poems

Ten Poems to Change Your Life Again and Again

Sacred Journeys in a Modern World

Ten Poems to Say Goodbye

Saved by Beauty: Adventures of an American Romantic in Iran

Twenty Poems to Bless Your Marriage

Keeping the Faith without Religion

DROPPING THE STRUGGLE

Seven Ways to Love the Life You Have

ROGER HOUSDEN

New World Library
Novato, California

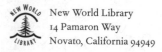 New World Library
14 Pamaron Way
Novato, California 94949

Text design by Tona Pearce Myers

Library of Congress Cataloging-in-Publication Data is available.

First printing, September 2016
ISBN 978-1-60868-406-9
Ebook ISBN 978-1-60868-407-6
Printed in Canada on 100% postconsumer-waste recycled paper

 New World Library is proud to be a Gold Certified Environmentally Responsible Publisher. Publisher certification awarded by Green Press Initiative. www.greenpressinitiative.org

10   9   8   7   6   5   4   3   2   1

CONTENTS

INTRODUCTION

Life, as we all know, is conflict, and man, being part of life, is himself an expression of conflict. If he recognizes the fact and accepts it, he is apt, despite the conflict, to know peace and to enjoy it. But to arrive at this end...a man has got to learn the doctrine of acceptance, that is, of unconditional surrender, which is love.

—— HENRY MILLER

HENRY MILLER IS SURELY RIGHT: life, as most of us experience it, often consists of challenge and conflict. We begin life by struggling to get here out of the womb, and that is just the beginning of a very long road. Sometimes we feel as if we are battling with odds that nearly always seem to be stacked against us. So you might think that dropping the struggle, as the title of this book suggests, means giving up on life, throwing in the towel in response to whatever challenge you are faced with. But Miller's thinking here doesn't take that route. It leads to the unconditional surrender of love. In the book you have in your hands, dropping the struggle leads not away from life but deeply into it.

The kind of surrender that Henry Miller points to is an echo of Nietzsche's idea, *amor fati*, loving your fate — acknowledging and accepting the conditions of your life exactly as they are, whatever they are — because that is what you have. This is not to say your fate cannot be changed — that's not what Nietzsche meant— no, he was saying that this moment right now is your fate. Each moment of your life offers you an opportunity to respond more creatively, more intelligently, than the last moment.

Yet how does loving the life you have — embracing it fully just as it is — become a natural experience day to day? That's the question this book invites you to live. I believe that you can only fully allow your current experience into your consciousness when, if only for a moment, something in you stops struggling with your experience, stops trying to make it other than what it is. You allow your full experience when you feel the space between your fear-based thoughts and let yourself rest there, where nothing ever is. Then a deeper knowing can move through you and emerge as needed into appropriate action.

This is what happened for writer and psychologist Rick Hanson when he was sixteen years old and working as a camp counselor near the Pacific Ocean. In his case, dropping the struggle became a matter of life and death.

> There was a lot of skin diving (without scuba gear) into the forests of kelp. One time I foolishly swam into a thicket of kelp, thinking there was clear water just on the other side. But there was only more sea-weed, with thick orangish leaves and long strong vines reaching up from the seabed below. I was trapped, running out of air, and began to panic. I battled the kelp, thrashing and jerking, which only wrapped it more tightly around me. After I don't know how long, a clarity came over me and my war with the kelp ended. My diving mask was around my throat, my snorkel ripped out of my mouth, and I'd lost a fin. I slowly disentangled myself from the kelp rather than fighting it, working my way upward, finally clearing it, seeing the bright silver surface of

the ocean above my head, and rising up to it and then the precious air.

"A clarity came over me," Hanson says. That clarity could not have come from his struggling mind; it must have surfaced from a deeper layer of intelligence, a layer not subject to the fear that generates our struggles, in whatever form they come. He did not *try* to generate a feeling of clarity; he dropped into it, as if it were already there, a calm quality of intelligence beneath the struggle. This is the open secret: each moment is an opportunity to know this calm clarity that Hanson speaks of. And yet each moment presents a paradox, because we can't *do* surrender as an act of will. We can't *decide* to embrace our experience. But in dropping our struggle we allow the space to open up to a deeper intelligence. This is what happened to Hanson at just the right moment.

Something similar happened to Ben Saunders, the polar explorer who set out unaided to complete Captain Scott's epic journey to the South Pole. Saunders undertook the longest unsupported polar expedition in human history — 1,800 miles, or the length of sixty-nine marathons back to back.

In an interview with Sarah Lewis, Saunders said, "Out

in the Arctic, I was aware that I was responsible for my own survival," but eventually he settled into a "wonderful feeling of 'Well, I can't think of a better word than surrender,'" as he described the process of nonresistance to wind, temperatures, and pain.

How do you lean into pain when you're trying to forge ahead in one of the most inhospitable places on the planet? And why is doing so helpful? To explain the essence of this kind of surrender, Lewis turns to the martial art of aikido, which derives its power from "strategic nonresistance." Aikido embodies the idea that when we stop resisting something, we stop giving it power. In aikido the person who receives an attack from the thrower absorbs and transforms the incoming energy through harmony and blending. There is no word for *competitor*, only for the one who is giving or receiving the energy.

What stands out in Saunders's story is his description of surrender as a "wonderful feeling." There he was, in the middle of nowhere, no one else within hundreds of miles, utterly at the mercy of the elements, his life in the balance. Surely nothing could be more frightening. Surely nothing would motivate him more to bend his head into the wind and push on with every ounce of strength left to him. Yet something in him knew to let go, to let go of all resistance to the reality of his situation. The nonresistance was itself the wonderful feeling.

Neither Hanson nor Saunders decided to love their fate, to let go of all resistance to their predicament. You can't *try* not to try, because letting go is not in the conscious mind's repertoire. But you can allow it. You can lean or fall back from conscious striving into a naked openness, a quality of being that is recognized by spiritual traditions the world over. Some call it spacious awareness, others the intelligence of the heart, or mind in the heart, while others call it the ever-present, aware stillness.

Neuroscience now provides an explanation for what happened to Hanson and Saunders, who both found themselves in intense physically taxing predicaments. In his book *Trying Not to Try*, Edward Slingerland discusses the research done by neuroscientist Arne Dietrich on the subduing of the cognitive control regions of the prefrontal cortex that occurs during strenuous physical workouts. Vigorous physical activity puts enormous stress on the body, and the body responds by temporarily shutting down parts deemed inessential, like our energy-hungry prefrontal cortex. Slingerland says that the resulting cognitive state looks very much like the relaxed, natural mind that Lao-tzu described in his *Tao Te Ching*, the principal text of Taoism. Slingerland goes

on to say that "timelessness, living in the here and now,...
peacefulness...are consistent with a state of frontal hypo-
function. Even abstruse feelings such as the unity with the
self and/or nature might be more explicable, considering
that the prefrontal cortex is the very structure that provides
us with the ability to segregate, differentiate, and analyze
the environment."

Whether or not they knew it, Saunders and Hanson
were acting on the famous advice of martial artist Bruce
Lee to "be like water." This is the exact opposite of what
eons of evolution have optimized our minds and bodies to
do — which is to tense up, snap into fight-or-flight mode,
and enlist all our willful resistance in a basic survival in-
stinct of self-protection.

Most of us are familiar with struggles far less dramatic
than bending one's head into an Arctic snowstorm or un-
tangling oneself from a kelp forest. Yet the same principle of neuroscience applies to our daily challenges. The
solution to most of life's predicaments — and especially
those that cannot be solved on a spreadsheet — does not
fall within the purview of the prefrontal cortex. It emerges
from a more unconscious — Lao-tzu would say more natural and spontaneous — dimension, one that joins us to a
larger field of awareness in which action unfolds organically

in response to the truth of the situation. Like Saunders in the snowy wastes, we finally acknowledge the truth of our situation, and we open our arms to it—not as a strategy to get us out of a tight corner but because we finally see that there is nothing else to do.

Until a few years ago I had spent the greater part of my time in a more or less covert struggle with life. However well things were going, I often felt that something was not quite right. Either I didn't want what turned up in quite the form it appeared, or I wanted something else that never quite materialized in the way I would have hoped. Always there was the pervasive feeling that something was missing, something I couldn't quite put my finger on.

So I struggled to find the missing piece. I struggled for meaning and ran all over India and the Middle East looking for it. I struggled to feel that I was somebody rather than nobody, I struggled to find creative work that inspired me, I struggled with the past and with concerns for the future, I struggled in relationships, I struggled to improve myself, and sometimes I even struggled to get out of bed in the morning instead of hiding under the sheets. And yes, I would struggle to avoid the fact that I am not built to last and that the whole Roger show would be over before I'd even had time to discover what on earth it was all about.

And yet for much of my life I wasn't even aware that I was struggling. It was so normal, and often so subtle — the background banter in my head as I went about my day — that I never even thought to call it a struggle; until, that is, I gradually became intimate enough with myself to acknowledge the feeling tones with which I moved through the day and to see through the ways I made my own life so needlessly difficult. Now the struggles are mostly over, or when they aren't, I manage to see them more quickly for what they are and remember — mostly — to step out of the ring. Call it the natural wisdom of aging if you like. If I have not learned to drop the struggle by now, I probably never will.

Struggle happens for all of us, so it must have a place in the scheme of things, but I for one have spent way too much time struggling for what struggle can never accomplish. *For struggle is not the same as effort* what is sometimes called "right effort." We all need to make an effort in every area of our life, effort that allows us to fulfill an intention or that edges us toward what we know to be true, even if we don't inhabit it now. Life doesn't just provide us with food and shelter as a natural right. Roger Federer didn't become the tennis champion he is without effort. If you are anything like me, you didn't make it through college without effort. Effort is a natural exertion of the personal will toward a specified end.

But struggle is an added push that is born of fear. Ultimately, it is born of the fear of not surviving, of dissolving and disappearing, not just as a physical form but as a psychological self. Struggle reinforces the ego's identity. It is one of the ways the ego asserts its existence.

Yet struggle will never get us the things we want most — love; meaning; presence; freedom from anxiety over the past and future; contentment with ourselves exactly as we are, imperfections and all; the acceptance of our mortality — because these things lie outside the ego's domain. For these, we need another way. That way begins and ends in surrender, in letting go of our resistance to life as it presents itself.

We struggle with reality when we lose touch with the dimension of our being that is not defined by our egoic identity. Who or what is larger than the ego? You are. This book is dedicated to that larger, indefinable you, to reminding you to rest back into the life you already have, just as it is. And I say "reminding you" because deep down we already know. It's easier than you think, but it takes more than an hour-long yoga class.

It takes an *allowing*, in the form of a persistent, deep,

and courageous Yes! to life right now. That Yes doesn't wave away the pain of the world as mere illusion; neither does it attempt to become some detached awareness or witness safely removed from the trials of life. It doesn't mean not caring about what happens in the world or in our own lives. It means caring so much that the heart spills open. It means being willing to be fully here where we are, wherever we are, however dark or light it happens to be.

When that Yes happens, we open our arms to life as it appears and disappears, moment to moment. We fall back into the larger aliveness that we already are, out of range of the ego's dictates. This is true relaxation; it is what we are here for. And it is what this book is for: to help you celebrate seven different ways of dropping the struggle and loving the life you already have.

A NOTE ON THE USE OF POETRY
AS A WISDOM LANGUAGE

IT MAY NOT SURPRISE those of you who have read any of my Ten Poems series to see that while this book you have in your hands is not about poetry, it uses poetry throughout to capture and illustrate the essence of dropping the struggle with life and allowing life to show us the way. Unlike spiritual traditions, whose language and customs, for all their profound wisdom, are culture and dogma bound, great poetry speaks truth in a universal language that crosses cultural boundaries and speaks directly to the human heart with a precision and force that prose can rarely aspire to.

Prose is invaluable as a means of explanation and argument; poetry, however, does not explain. It goes straight to the heart of an experience and delivers it, at its best, in the form of a precise and essential truth that human beings anywhere can recognize. It is inspired utterance, not a teaching, and we do not recognize its truth with the prefrontal cortex. This is what the poet Wallace Stevens meant when he said that poetry "must resist the intelligence almost successfully."

It is the knowing heart that can recognize the truth in a great poem. It is that same knowing heart that prompts a deeper response to life than struggle. This is why I have chosen to use the language of poetry throughout the book.

DROPPING THE STRUGGLE
TO BE SPECIAL

Release

Does it matter who I am?
To have a Definition
to make me stand out
or blend in
to have a set Life Plan.

Walking in the storm
sky breaking overhead
it is easier if "I" am simply here
on the pavement walking
in the company of leaves
blowing about.

It is easier if I am not Someone
fighting against the wind
talking to myself about how
soaked my new boots are getting
kicking myself for not bringing
an umbrella.

If I don't have to be Someone
I don't have anything to cling to
or defend.

This used to scare me
I can't be nothing!
I can't be no one!

But now?
Give me Nobody
over Somebody
any day.

After the storm
the leaves will settle,
fall where they will,
their curled browned
bodies will greet us
in the morning

drops of grace
on our way to school and work.

A colleague asks me,
Hey, what's new?
and I reply,
Everything.

— TAMMY HANNA

TAMMY HANNA IS A SCHOOLTEACHER living in London. Her poem, which she submitted in one of my online writing classes, reminds me that deep insight can be attained anywhere, at any time, and by anyone. You don't have to be a Rumi or a spiritual teacher or an adventurer in the Arctic to drop the struggle with life and fall into the freedom that is always present. Tammy found it on a London street while walking home from school. Neither do you have to be interrogated by the Iranian Intelligence Service.

In 2009 I was in Iran to research a book on the culture and people. After two months there I was on my way out of the country, when I was stopped by members of the Iranian Intelligence Service at the airport. They took me back to Tehran and interrogated me for two days under suspicion of being a spy. For a while it looked as if I would never see home again.

As an educated English white male, I had gone through life with a certain degree of entitlement, unconsciously exuding an air that seemed to imply I had a special pass. This is partly personal, but it is also part of my collective inheritance. English men have strutted the globe for centuries feeling special, and even though any justification for such a posture has long since disintegrated — even though it was never justified in the first place — the feeling lingers on through the generations. It's a core cultural belief, and those change only slowly. So I can be as full of myself as anyone.

I admit it didn't look good, that afternoon in Tehran. I had met all the wrong people — dissident artists, reformist politicians, and Sufi sheikhs in Kurdistan, where tourists were not meant to go. My interrogators knew everything because they had hacked into my email account and listened to every phone call I had made. They knew I was not a tourist and that I was writing a book. Somehow, entirely by serendipity — being passed from one friendly pair of Iranian hands to another — I had been invited to Christmas dinner with the English ambassador at the embassy, and the chargé d'affaires at the Swiss Embassy, who was responsible for American affairs in Iran, had thrown a party for me the night before I left for the airport, in a diplomatic car that she insisted I take — for my own protection, she said.

Throughout my time in Iran, it had felt as if the gods were smiling on me. Until the moment I was stopped by the agents, my life had always been marked by a certain naïveté that allowed me to glide through situations and countries without being harmed. It was a kind of grace that I had never really been conscious of until it seemed about to be taken away.

After two days of being asked the same questions again and again — Who sent you here, Who are you working for, Why did you come to the airport in a diplomatic car, What were you doing in Kurdistan? — my interrogators, two burly men in baggy black suits, finally stopped talking. One of them began cracking his knuckles. The other held up my English passport and said, "You see this? This is worthless! Do you realize you could disappear today and no one would ever know?"

That was becoming all too evident. He threw my passport into the wastebasket. So much for my English special pass.

"Have you ever heard of Evin Prison?"

I had heard of Evin, and I did not like what I heard. The man who threw my passport away glared at me.

"You are very fortunate," he said. "My colleague is the boss and he is going to give you a choice. You can either spend a minimum of five years in Evin Prison, or you can work for us as an informant on the activities of foreign NGOs in Iran."

I said I would work for them. I was told to stand by the boss and shake his hand with a smile while the other man took our photograph.

"We will cause trouble for you with this if you do not follow through," he said. The two men rose as if on cue and left the room, saying they would be back in five minutes.

I went to the balcony and looked down at the lights of the city below. I was on the fourteenth floor. It was the middle of the night. My life was at a turning point. There was no way out of this. I had grown up in a liberal democracy, in which fairness and justice were considered fundamental values. I had always assumed that no harm could come, which is probably why I so blithely got on a plane to Iran in the first place, to the country that both England and America, the countries that had issued my two passports, were calling part of the Axis of Evil.

But there in Iran it was plain that I was no different from anyone else: from the journalists who were already in Evin Prison, from the Berkeley students who had been caught straying over the Iraqi-Iranian border around the same time, from the thousands of people all over the world who had lost their freedom for no apparent reason. I realized that everything could be taken away from me at any moment. Whatever feeling of specialness I had carried around with me fell away in that room high over Tehran.

I was helpless. I felt a gravitas, an emerging humility that I had not known before. Something in me gave up. Gave up worrying, gave up thinking about possible outcomes, gave up everything. I waited. Ten minutes passed. Half an hour. I peered out of the window at the lights of the city below. For all I knew, I could be somewhere in this city for years. Maybe this was it for my life. Maybe it would end here. An hour passed, and in that hour I came to know three things, and not with my thinking mind.

First, I knew that even as I was part of a web of loving relationships that I cherished, I was at the same time utterly alone. Existentially, essentially alone, as one dies. As one may be upon hearing a cancer diagnosis or upon surviving a car crash. No one was sharing this turn of events in Tehran with me. No one even knew where I was.

The second thing I knew beyond all doubt was that the narrative I had assumed to be my identity was a fabrication spun out of my neurons. Roger the traveler, the writer, the lover of poetry — all this was a provisional reality. My memories, too, were shifting and subject to change. In that room in Tehran, all my usual reference points had drifted away. The familiar story of my life meant nothing in my present circumstances.

And yet, and yet, the very absence of my well-worn identity felt like a sudden breath of freedom, like taking off a tight suit I had not even realized I was wearing. Part of the stitching holding the suit together was the unconscious feeling that I was somehow exempt from the usual restrictions. It was a defense, of course, and ludicrous if I cared to look at it. The Iranians had seen through my game. Now I understood that line of Rumi's, from his poem "Time to Go Home," in which he says that we can walk around without clothes on:

Let's leave grazing to cows and go
Where we know what everyone really intends,
Where we can walk around without clothes on.

(TRANSLATED BY COLEMAN BARKS)

Even terms like *alone* and *not alone*, *free* and *unfree*, *English* and *American* didn't make sense without my usual identity. Yet in this nakedness, not knowing anything about my life from here on out, something essential continued to palpitate, to throb beneath my skin. I am! Whatever happens, I realized then, I am; I am nothing to speak of, no one special at all, just the silence of clear air. Feeling this in that room in Tehran was the greatest freedom I had known. *This* was my true home, a home without walls.

Whether I live or die, whatever happens, *I am* — I saw and felt this as clear as day. None of it was a thought; it was a felt sensation, a knowing beyond words. I felt intensely alive, not with excitement, but with a deep and solid and sober peace. My curiosity reemerged. I wondered what the next chapter in the story would be. There would always be a story until there wasn't, even though I knew now with a visceral certainty that however the story turned out, it wouldn't define who I was in essence, which was ungraspable.

It's not that I didn't have preferences. Of course I wanted my freedom. Really wanted it. But I could also feel a calm and sober detachment about whatever might happen next. The story that unfolded might not be the story I thought I was going to live. And in some inexplicable way, even that would be alright. I would continue to be, whatever happened.

Then the door opened, and the two men in baggy suits walked in. We are going to the airport, they said. You will be on the next flight to Dubai. And I was. And for the record, I do not work for the Iranian Intelligence Service.

Even telling this story could be a way for me to feel good about myself, to feel that an unusual experience validates my feeling of being somebody special. The ego can twist itself into any shape it likes and believe it is being authentic. We can even turn being nobody special into a spiritual costume that the ego slips into when no one is looking.

There is an old Jewish story of two rabbis walking through the synagogue, when they spot the cleaner mumbling to himself. They could just catch his words: "Adonai, have mercy, for I am no one, not even a speck in your eye." One rabbi leaned into the other and in a tone of disdain, said in his ear, "Look who thinks *he* is nobody."

The rabbis felt superior to the cleaner. After all, they were rabbis. What could the cleaner know about the spiritual virtue of humility? Or at a deeper level, beyond the virtue of humility, how could a mere cleaner see through his ego's story to the luminous silence that is everywhere? Because this is what being nobody really means: living without a central operating system with your name tag on it.

True humility can be a gateway to such a way of living. Seeing ourselves in proportion, as one among many, softens our boundaries and makes us more susceptible to a deeper knowing. Most of us try to feel superior at times by comparing ourselves with someone who, either in character, profession, or knowledge, we judge to be less than us. Comparison is one of the ways the ego solidifies itself — either by making us feel special or small, which are two sides of the same coin. Thomas Jefferson captured this in one succinct sentence:

Remember that no one is better than you, but that you are better than no one.

Of course, any healthy ego enjoys being valued, praised, given unsolicited special treatment, looked up to in some way. We don't have to be narcissists to enjoy feeling special. The trouble comes when we identify with the praise, with our eminent position or knowledge — when we begin to believe that the shiny image is who we are and that we deserve special regard or treatment because of it. Then the warm feeling of being appreciated becomes grandiosity.

There's something entirely beautiful and appropriate about polishing a talent or skill. There's something truly gratifying about doing anything well. Civilization owes a great debt to all those who have been willing to dedicate their lives to a talent or cause that has raised the bar of what it means to be human. Nelson Mandela, Rosa Parks, the Dalai Lama, Yo Yo Ma, Beethoven, Tolstoy, Emily Dickinson, Pablo Neruda,

Marie Curie — the list of exceptional individuals is endless. People like this are indeed special.

They were given a gift from the gods and it would be easy, forgivable, even, for it to go to their heads, but there are some who possess great skill without taking it personally. They have worked and given their lives to a talent or a cause, but they know that the creative or spiritual power for which they have served as a conduit is not theirs to claim. Many of these individuals know what most of us do not: that the more you know, the more you realize how little you know; the more you give yourself to a discipline, the more you realize how little of the road you have traveled.

In 1913, just six years before the end of his long life, Pierre-Auguste Renoir, the great French Impressionist painter, said, "I am just learning to paint."

Yet you can't *try* to experience humility, because humility is an authentic quality of being that cannot be imitated by the ego. You can't *try* to live as if you know you are no more or less than anyone else. Most of us have to be humbled, brought to our knees by the trials of life. The struggles call us to surrender our positions, our ideas of who we are and how life was meant to be. Humility emerges when life returns us to our proportionate place in the scheme of things; when we are willing and able to witness ourselves without blame or judgment as we really are, warts and all; or because by grace we are grounded in a dimension of our humanity that is already below the surface of our story.

It's not easy to know humility as long as we believe our own story. If we are only our story, our image, we need to feel special in order to feel substantial; because deep down we know we have no ground. Something in us knows that the identity we create to move through the world is always and only ever provisional, not just because we die but also because we can intuit that it has no solid foundation throughout our lifetime. For all its valuable executive powers, the ego identity is only more or less useful in helping us make our way in the world. Of course it has value: we all need a story to live in this world. We all need to be someone to fill out a job application.

But if we are lucky, the time will come when life will turn us upside down and all our precious coins will fall out of our pockets. If you practice Zen, the same might happen if you sit in front of a white wall for a day or for ten years, when your whole house of cards suddenly falls to the ground and you recognize the shimmering silence that you are and always were. Or you look in the mirror one day while you are brushing your teeth and suddenly see through all your joy and sorrow to the one who is looking, the stillness in the midst of the big wind of your life. In the hero's journey, the time must come when the hero encounters so great a pressure, inside or out, that something has to give. He or she is the one who has to give — give up the very notion of being a hero on a journey, and fall facedown onto the earth. There is never any guarantee of a happy ending, and because this is so, a door might swing open that we never even knew was there.

Experiences such as surrender, acceptance, and allowing will never work as strategies. You can't fake it, just as you can't pretend not to feel special, as the rabbis in our story show us all too clearly. Yet you can be willing to watch the ego at work, to notice what it feels like when you compare yourself, placing yourself above or below someone. Eventually, one day or moment — who knows why? — the heart door will spring open and there you are in another land; there you are, a curl of mist on the wind.

To be as mysterious and ungraspable as a curl of mist on the wind — that is exactly what the ego is frightened of. It doesn't want to be a curl of mist on the wind; it wants to feel its own gravitas, its own authority and power to act. That's what it struggles for, and the struggle itself gives it a feeling of existence. Take the struggle away, and who or what would our identity be? Suffering makes up a large part of most people's identity, which is one reason it is difficult to give up. After all, if we give up the struggle to become someone, who will we be? What will we be?

My ego had nowhere to turn in that room in Tehran. Without any means of escape, it had no option other than to let go. It had no answer to my situation, which is why a deeper knowing could emerge — the knowing that *I am* no matter what, completely independent of my life story as I tell it. The truth is that the ego *never* has an answer to any question or paradox that really matters. The only answer is to surrender.

What we surrender to is the vivid aliveness that is already there behind all we think we know, behind all the arguments and reasons we have for everything. And we fall back into the clarity of that unknowing by surrendering to the present moment, to what is already happening, inside and out. Just as it is in this moment. It's both impossible and simple — we just need the presence of mind to unhook ourselves from the story we are making up about the present moment and let it be what it is. Thankfully, not everyone has to be locked up in a room in Tehran with two scowling security agents in baggy black suits to get the message that Tammy Hanna received on a London street one day and poured into the poem at the beginning of this chapter.

DROPPING THE STRUGGLE
FOR A PERFECT LIFE

From "Relax"

Bad things are going to happen....
No matter how many vitamins you take,
how much Pilates, you'll lose your keys,
your hair and your memory....
Your wallet will be stolen, you'll get fat,
slip on the bathroom tiles of a foreign hotel
and crack your hip. You'll be lonely.
Oh taste how sweet and tart
the red juice is, how the tiny seeds
crunch between your teeth.

— ELLEN BASS

YOU MAY HAVE NOTICED that sometimes — no, more often than not — the day, the week, your life, turns out other than you had expected, and not always for the better. No matter how much we try to do the right thing, become a better or more spiritual person, get all our ducks in a row at work, at home, or with our friends, something always seems to show up to remind us that this is not a perfect world and that it never will be. Something always shows us that, no matter how smart we are or how many successes we have under our belt, we do not have ultimate control for the way our life works out, not to mention for the way the world works out.

I imagine that some experience of this truth is what prompted Ellen Bass to write her poem. And since unexpected misfortune, as well as luck, seems to be sewn into the fabric of life, we might as well relax and keep on breathing. Life is imperfect, however much we pretend otherwise. It doesn't always live up to our expectations. But then, we are imperfect, and our family and friends are imperfect, and we and they don't always live up to our expectations, either. No one is in charge of how life turns out.

But it's not easy to relax when we imagine that the world has it in for us when things don't go the way we want or expect, when we think that there must be something wrong with us, that we must have been born under an unlucky star to have deserved the trouble we find ourselves in. It's not easy when we take life personally, and most of us do, most of the time. But it's not personal; it really isn't. We're not that important. The world existed for 4.6 billion years before we came here and will likely continue for at least that amount of time after we have disappeared.

Life just works out the way it does, and none of us really knows why we do what we do at any given time. Nobody knows why the pot falls from the shelf or the sink clogs up just as our dinner guests are knocking at the door. We never really know why our friend or lover shouts at us, disappears, or is suddenly filled with undying love for us. *They* don't even know! It's always a good idea to listen to Rilke, who wrote: "Let life happen to you. Believe me: life is in the right, always."

Jack Kornfield put it this way:

One day Ajahn Chah held up a beautiful Chinese teacup. "To me this cup is already broken. Because I know its fate, I can enjoy it fully here and now. And when it's gone, it's gone." When we understand the truth of uncertainty and relax, we become free.

The broken cup helps us see beyond our illusion of control. When we commit ourselves to raising a child, building a business, creating a work of art, or righting an injustice, some measure of failure as well as success will be ours. This is a fierce teaching. Emilee is an aid worker whose clinic in Kosovo was burned to the ground, yet she began again. She knows that her work is helping people through success and failure. Rosa, who lost her most promising math student to a gang shooting, was brokenhearted. But she doesn't regret having tutored him, and now she is tutoring several others in his honor.

We may lose our best piece of pottery in the firing, the charter school we work so hard to create may fold, our start-up business may go under, our children may develop problems beyond our control. If we focus only on the results, we will be devastated. But if we know the cup is broken, we can give our best to the process, create what we can, and trust the larger process of life itself. We can plan, care for, tend, and respond. But we cannot control. Instead we take a breath, and open to what is unfolding, where we are. This is a profound shift, from holding on, to letting go.

Everything and everyone in our lives, including ourselves, is already going the way of that broken teacup. Day by day tiny specks of us float away. Nothing can dispel the reality that we are not built to last. Death is our ultimate limitation, the final proof that perfection was never meant to be part of the human experience. Sooner or later we will not be here: no eyes, no nose, no ears, no tongue, no mind, no you or me — gone, and who knows where?

The fantasy of control, of the effectiveness of our decisions, is at the heart of Western culture. The struggle to take charge of our life and improve both ourselves and our condition is part of the mythos of American society. It doesn't end with an impressive degree or a move up the social or financial ladder. We practice brain games to improve our mental agility, we work out in the gym to tone the body, we work with a therapist to smooth out our psychological knots, we work on improving our meditation, and we also work toward a better world.

All this effort is laudable and worthy. It feels good to be at the helm of our life. The rub comes when, often without knowing it, we turn our lives into a project with the assumption that something is inherently wrong with us and that with enough determination and focus we can fix it. The ultimate perfection fantasy is a spiritual one: with enough meditation or spiritual practice we can fly free of all the usual human imperfections, dissolve all our attachments, and reach enlightenment, whatever that means. The Tibetan trickster teacher Chögyam Trungpa called this "spiritual materialism." And the trouble with this approach is that the one doing the trying is the same one who needs to step out of the way in the first place.

The Christian West, with its concept of original sin, is founded on the idea that something is inherently wrong with us. We had to have someone die in order to save us from our sins. We have been reaping the consequences of that belief in a thousand different ways ever since. Essentially, we labor under the assumption that something is not well with the world and with ourselves — and that it's our fault! So of course we have to strive to make ourselves worthy, to make ourselves spiritual and whole.

Yet there is another view, common in the Zen and Taoist traditions, that insists we are already perfect exactly as we are — blemishes and all. In ancient China holy rascals like Lao-tzu and Chuang-tzu (a follower of Lao-tzu) assured us that everything is already as it needs to be. In *The Second Book of the Tao*, Chuang-tzu wrote,

Let go of all your assumptions
And the world will make perfect sense.

We are perfect as we are when we can acknowledge that our imperfections, whatever they may be, are part of the larger picture of who we are. But it's not just a matter of sitting back and saying, after some outburst or reaction, *Well, that's just how I am. I was made that way and it's perfect just as it is.* What Lao-tzu and friends meant by *perfection* is that whatever arises in our life, from within or from without, is arising. It's happening, and therefore has to happen — because it just did! That is why even our obscurations and blind spots are perfect — they have appeared, like it or not. When something appears in our consciousness, we have three choices:

1. *closed mind*: Ignore it.
2. *lost mind*: Identify with the thought and the feeling and respond as if it were true.
3. *open mind*: Experience the thought and feeling without judgment or fear, and know it for what it is, a narrative imposed on reality and not the truth about reality.

I for one can still be upended by a thought or a feeling that will dog me for hours, snapping at my heels, insisting I not only listen to it but acknowledge the truth it is trying to convince me of. Some years ago I went to a talk on a classic of English literature, and I found myself almost instantly feeling an aversion to the speaker's ebullient, extroverted style. Underneath I could also sense that I felt contracted and inadequate in the face of his learning. I felt lacking in formal academic knowledge, even though I presumed to give talks similar to the one I was listening to. Why hadn't I buckled down and taken that extra degree in my earlier life? Aware of my aversion, I tried to connect with the spaciousness I had known in meditation earlier in the day. Essentially, I tried to ignore my actual experience and substitute a feeling that might help me feel better. I wasn't very successful. I could have remembered Rilke.

> Why do you want to shut out of your life any uneasiness, any misery, any depression, since after all you don't know what work these conditions are doing inside you?

But I didn't remember Rilke. I was so distracted that at the end of the lecture I left my satchel by my chair, complete with the thumb drive containing my own presentation that I was due to deliver the next morning. I called the host when I got home, only to discover that she had already left and I wouldn't be able to retrieve my satchel for a week.

Only then did I remember that whatever is going on in my head is always, but always, an inside job. My aversion, I realized, had nothing to do with the person I had been listening to. It was fueled by my own sense of inadequacy, my own version of a hole in the middle. That, and not anything about the lecturer, was the truth of the moment, but at the time I wasn't able to embrace that fact. So during the lecture I had stewed in the reverberations of all these thoughts that were hanging on to each other's tails and threatening to form a noose round my neck.

Forgetting my satchel was the catalyst that showed me my condition. I sat down with myself and let myself feel. I let myself open to the bodily sensations of feeling underqualified, poorly prepared for the next day's two-hour presentation. I felt illegitimate, and that connected back to a vein that has run through my life, since I was born "illegitimate." There was no need to follow a story about the feelings that were there; what I needed was simply to let myself feel them, beyond their names, down into the visceral contraction — feel them while not losing touch with the larger spaciousness that I also knew to be there.

The error I had initially made — one that is all too easy

to make — was attempting to control the impact of my uncomfortable thoughts through bypassing them and replacing them with a feeling of spaciousness and calm. I know it doesn't work that way; I know that both realities need to be embraced, but sometimes I forget. The only way through is to accept the gift of the moment, however it shows up. If what shows up is inadequacy, or illegitimacy, let it be so. This too. These moments were offering me the opportunity to accept my vulnerabilities and fragility. It's this simple: I am not required to hold it together all the time. Unless and until I can embrace my imperfections, my incapacity in the face of life's immensity, I will never be free of judging the imperfections of others. As for my own lecture the following day, it turned out to be far better — more able to fly free in its own authentic way — without the notes.

~

It is our limitations that make each of us human and the unique individuals that we are. Being limited and imperfect, we can count on making mistakes. However cautious and responsible we are, we are still bound to err. We take the wrong job, we choose the wrong partner, we bet on the wrong horse, we buy when we should have sold, we have one drink too many. However self-aware we may be, we will say something out of turn, cut someone off, assert our position in order to claim privilege.

We are simply never in charge of what appears in our mind or in our world moment to moment. Instead of trying to control our experience, judging it as good or bad, spiritual or base, life calls us to accept it as our present-moment reality — not pushing it away, giving in to it, or getting lost in it, but exploring it by surrendering to the truth of our experience. Speaking of his Zen practice, Barry Magid, teacher and author of *Ending the Pursuit of Happiness*, shares a rare insight that you don't often find in spiritual circles:

> There is this element of just surrendering to the moment that's built into the form and discipline of practice. That can make a big difference in our lives. But that takes you only so far, and then we have to go onto a next stage in which we bring back into our practice a deep acceptance of our own needs, desires, and vulnerabilities. We no longer think that practice in some way is going to extirpate them from our lives. This is particularly tricky, because we often see — or have been taught — that these feelings are the source of our unhappiness. There are too many

people who try to use practice as a way to diminish their vulnerabilities, their need for others, and their desire for moral support and security. These things are sometimes dismissed as attachments, and there's an unconscious ideal of self-sufficiency or autonomy in a lot of practices. Even though we're told about interdependence all the time, it's rarely described as emotional interdependence.

Most Buddhist teachings hold that our egoic identity is rooted in self-cherishing, meaning the constant practice of shoring up one's game by trying to feel good about oneself, turning a blind eye to one's own faults, and seeing the speck in the other's eye. But that evening after the lecture, I realized that what I really needed *was* in fact self-cherishing — but the kind Barry Magid describes — the kind that means deep acceptance of my vulnerabilities, without trying to sidestep them either with some form of rationalization or with an attempt to obscure them with a more pleasant and spacious experience.

It's so simple, really: it means being kind to ourselves. Being willing to accept whatever appears without judgment is to extend loving-kindness to ourselves in our imperfections, in our vulnerability, in our early childhood responses to current situations. This is what Ellen Bass points to in her poem: "Oh taste how sweet and tart the red juice is." She is pointing to the juice of our daily mishaps, misunderstandings, upended expectations — both sweet and tart, when we allow ourselves to fully taste them. Funny how the simplest things can be the most difficult. If we have the presence of mind to crunch those moments between our teeth so that we can taste how sweet and tart they are, something softens in us, and we return to ourselves.

Carl Jung wrote,

The one who learns to live with his incapacity has learned a great deal. This will lead us to the valuation of the smallest things, and to wise limitation, which the greater height demands.... The heroic in you is the fact that you are ruled by the thought that this or that is good, that this or that performance is indispensable,... this or that goal must be attained in headlong striving work, this or that pleasure should be ruthlessly repressed at all costs. Consequently you sin against incapacity. But incapacity exists. No one should deny it, find fault with it, or shout it down.

Sometimes surrender happens by grace, for no reason. The veils fall away from our eyes and we stand, blinking, in a new dawn. More often surrender follows a difficult struggle, one that can even be a matter of life or death, as we saw with Rick Hanson and Ben Saunders. It might be a struggle in everyday life or a spiritual struggle, a desperate desire to find union with God that ends in despair or hopelessness. It might be a psychological struggle.

Jung went through a prolonged internal conflict in which he was frightened of losing control of himself and becoming prey to the dark fantasies that were filling his mind, until he realized that there was no way out but to let himself drop. *Suddenly it was as if the ground literally gave way beneath my feet, and I plunged down into dark depths...*

Jung was afraid of losing command and yet had to take the chance, so he chose to let himself drop and suddenly plunged down. He emerged with an extraordinary aliveness and creativity, which took form in what came to be *The Red Book.*

We feel more alive when we finally come home to who we are in our entirety — not to some manicured and spiritualized image but to who we are as we show up, moment by moment. Here we sense a silent, aware space that allows all our experiences to pass through it like so many weather systems. That deep acceptance — not a grudging acceptance but a celebration — of who we are arises not from the ego itself but from that spacious awareness. Knowing this is the cure for spiritual homesickness. It is when we begin to realize that what we have been hankering for has been there all along.

DROPPING THE STRUGGLE
FOR MEANING AND PURPOSE

I said to the wanting-creature inside me:
What is this river you want to cross?...
Do you believe there is some place that will make the
soul less thirsty?
In that great absence you will find nothing.

— KABIR,
translated by Robert Bly

"EVERY MAN SHALL BE HIS OWN PRIEST," Walt Whitman said. Yet the freedom to minister to our own souls — to find our own source of value and meaning rather than have it be prescribed by social or religious orthodoxy — is not easily won. The pressure is strong — both from within and without — to find meaning in the objective, exterior world. Our culture exhorts us to become someone, rather than to be someone, by building a list of concrete achievements, by making a mark that will somehow defeat the flow of time. It encourages us to find meaning from outer roles and actions rather than resting back in the inherent value of our own interiority, rather than turning the gaze around and letting it rest on the seer rather than on what is seen.

Of course, the process of becoming is what generates both our human adventure and the adventure of the entire cosmos. Everything is always becoming. Being is always becoming. Life itself is making us all up as we go along. But life is always more meaningful and yes, more simple, when our activities and roles — the signatures of becoming — come from a deeper source than the strategizing, anxious self, when they carry the authentic tone of who we are without any role or function, prior even to the accumulation of our life experience.

When that happens, life just happens. Events unfold naturally. Life flows through us because we ourselves have become a flow of being-into-becoming rather than a solid subject clinging to some cherished fixed identity.

If you read an obituary, you will see that a person's life is almost entirely described by her outer achievements. The implication is that these achievements are the sum of that person's value and the source of her meaning. When you write your own obituary, however, you are more likely to see yourself from the inside out. I recently asked my writing students to write their own obituaries, and I completed the exercise myself. These are some of the paragraphs that appeared on my obituary page:

> *Fire in the Heart*, his first book was called, and whether he knew it or not, it was that fire that was the guiding motif of his life. A fire that burned lightly inside his chest, a passionate loving of living that when he was joined to it joined him to the world and all that is in it.
>
> Joined to it he was sometimes not, however, and for much of his life that fire raised smoke in the form of a search for meaning and purpose; a search that

was never satisfied by the conventional avenues to fulfillment and that led him to a lifelong questing for answers in the world's spiritual traditions. For many years he had a classic case of Seeker's Disease — the holy grail was always somewhere else. The illness caused him and those around him considerable angst, especially in his earlier years, and he was often so absorbed in his own wonderings and dreaming that he could often be absent while present with his son and his first wife.

He would sporadically feel a dizzying dark hole in his center that at times would render him helpless, unable to know what to do next. He would feel lacking in something he had no name for. He associated it with a lack of meaningful activity. Is this all there is? Surely I should be doing something more, contributing more. How best can I live this life? These questions were his frequent companions in the first half of his life, and they rarely came paired with answers; but he knew that the source of his lack was deeper than any external cause.

For years, then, nothing was ever quite enough; no one was ever quite enough. He himself was especially not enough, because he felt he was not living the fullness of life — although he had no idea what that meant. Yet as he began to stop fleeing from it — as he began to allow without resistance the gnawing in the pit of his stomach that no meal could satisfy — it slowly revealed itself to be the fertile ground he had always been looking for without knowing it.

It was as if he had been looking up at the night sky and instead of being enchanted by the stars had finally gazed into the fathomless dark out of which they and everything had come. Gradually, the more he relaxed into the stillness beyond all outer roles and identities, into the stillness of the presence of being, the empty void became a fruitful void, a loving aware presence that was to become the most intimate and wordless sense of meaning he would ever know.

Down through the years he fell in love with several women, and these intimacies were to prove foundational to opening his inner and emotional life. He was softened by them, brought into his humanity by them, into his vulnerability and tenderness. His feelings for women opened another doorway to the transcendent, which he had no name for other than Being.

Toward the end of his life he came to appreciate the gifts and the beauty of ordinary human existence, and found his deepest meaning and most luminous moments there. He left behind the longing for the extraordinary, the exceptional, the dramatic experiences that had taken him through the Sahara, all over India, and the Middle East and was nourished instead by deep and loving friendships, the daily blessings of nature, and most of all by the stillness of Being.

His books were all celebrations of the beauty, the fallibility, and the poignancy of human existence as known through his own existence; and celebrations, too, of the ever-presence of grace and mystery in the midst of life's ignorance and suffering. One of his later books was aptly called *Dropping the Struggle*. Loving the life he had been given was what he was finally doing.

Meaning, then, and its cousin, purpose — the wrestling with it, the struggles with it — has been a constant motif in my life. I remember a painting by Rembrandt of Jacob wrestling with the angel. It was like that somehow, the struggling to give a name and direction to that invisible thing that makes the difference between a corpse and a breathing human being; struggling to find ground in a life that is inevitably groundless since everything, even the stars, eventually falls away.

Leo Tolstoy suffered a similar struggle. Few individuals were ever as tormented by meaninglessness as was Tolstoy. He stands as a towering example of how success, wealth, and fame do not fill the hole in the middle. When he was fifty years old, at the peak of his success, Tolstoy found himself in what he called a crisis of "life arrest." What was the point, he asked himself, of managing his vast estates, of educating his son? What for? And what was the point of his writing? "What if I should be more famous than Gogol, Pushkin, Shakespeare, Molière — than all the writers in the world — well, and what then? I could find no reply."

He felt the foundations on which his life had been built crumbling away. "There was nothing left for me to stand on, that what I had been living for was nothing, that I had no reason for living . . . the truth was, life was meaningless." Tolstoy's dark night eventually became the doorway to a spiritual transformation, a plunge into being that allowed him to found a utopian community built on the principles of peace and faith — not faith in any particular religion but an existential faith in the goodness of life as it is.

The movement toward personal meaning — the level of becoming, or individuation — is usually associated with having a purpose, with the journey of becoming some- one through action and some form of achievement in the world, whether it be raising a child, launching a business, or performing an act of service. Find your purpose, and your meaning will follow, the idea goes, because purpose can bring a sense of order into what might otherwise feel like a random jumble of events.

I once took a workshop in which we were asked to define our purpose. I sat there for a few moments with the usual tropes running through my mind, but nothing seemed to fit. I was stumped. Then I realized that I saw purpose in a way that was intrinsically different from flow charts and graphs.

I could not say how my purpose was distinct from whatever I was doing or not doing in the moment. If there was a pattern to my life, in terms of my activities and my relationship to the world, I experienced it as a secret that was revealing itself to me moment by moment, step by step. It has never been the result of a five-year plan.

It was a secret because it was not accessible to my conscious mind. It lay deeper than that, and sometimes it secreted its perfume and sometimes it didn't. That's why systems and maps prescribed by others are unlikely to catch our scent on the wind: because our deeper purpose leaves a trace that only we can recognize.

The pattern of our existence — our original template, you could say — may emerge in the form of some vague prompting, or as a genuine delight, or as an affinity for a particular activity. It might be the moment when long-held values finally translate into action, as happened for Jena Lee Nardella. She left college with an overwhelming desire to bring a thousand wells to African villages. She was motivated by her Christian faith and by a spontaneous desire to respond to the needs of others.

The result was Blood: Water, an organization that has brought water to millions of people all over Africa. Jena started out with the desire to change the world. Ten years later, having experienced firsthand both the brokenness and the beauty in our human condition, she realized that her deepest purpose was not, after all, to change the world but to love it. Her work became less driven by results. She relaxed into an appreciation and an acceptance of the process along the way.

You might find your true purpose — your particular, authentic expression of being — through a serendipitous encounter. It might come as an intuition, some coincidence or sudden memory, like a reminder, apparently unrelated to your situation. However it comes, however fleetingly, it will feel significant. It may seem trivial, but that moment may be significant in a way that a major life event turns out not to be. Our job then is to listen, to listen and catch the lilt in the voice of the wind.

Many Western cultures hold that each individual has his own unique calling or pattern of potentiality that he is born with. The Greeks called it your *daimon*, the Romans called it your genius, the Christians your guardian angel. The Romantics, like John Keats, believed the call comes from the heart. It is both within you and also not in you. It is the pattern of your unique existence that you are called on to decipher. It is the seed you were born with that wants to bear fruit, and it carries your fate.

There is no one and never will be anyone just like you. *That is why your life, however it shows up, is your unique purpose.* Whatever is happening, whatever you are doing, that is the expression of your purpose right now. So look around you. *Your unfolding life is your gift to the world.* It is a gift that no one else can offer.

But that doesn't mean our individual story is already written and our life just lives itself out. It doesn't mean there is an unalterable script somewhere deep in our bones. That would be fatalism. It would be to say that everything is in the hands of the gods, that all we have to do is to sit back and see what happens. But no. Everything is in play until the very end. We live the paradox: our life will always be a mystery, imponderable; and it will always be our responsibility.

The word *fate* in the ancient Greek meant "a portion." Fate is only a portion of what happens, not, as fatalism would have it, the whole enchilada. The Greek idea of fate, rather than fatalism, is this: stuff happens. It happens in the convergence of different forces. Fate has a portion, a part, to play. Our personal energy, our authentic core, is also a portion. The context, the situation we are in, is another portion. The confluence of these forces at any one moment is expressed today as chaos theory. Life comes to us and through us out of left field. We are not in charge.

Fate, that irrational principle, swooped like a swallow at twilight into the life of Braeda Horan one evening in London. As a small child Braeda had loved to design clothes for the fairies, cutting them out of fallen leaves. Then when she was sixteen a leaflet appeared out of nowhere on her desk at her private straight-laced convent school in England saying that applications were open for a new design course at a famous art college.

"To this day I have no idea how that leaflet could have

found its way to my desk," she told me. "Nothing like it was ever seen in my school, which was exclusively geared to getting girls into Oxford or Cambridge. But when I saw it, I knew — even though I was under the normal admission age, and even though the entrance competition would be fierce — that I would leave school for that art college. My teachers were furious and told me I would be wasting my life."

Three years later, Braeda left the art school with honors, the youngest student at the college. She was offered a prestigious clothing design job in London, got a mews house in Knightsbridge and an original MINI Cooper, and joined the upper-class world of the swinging London of the seventies.

Within two years she felt empty and lost. She had everything anyone could want, and yet she felt her life lacked any real meaning. Most people at that time with a similar affliction headed off to India, but Braeda had heard tales for years from her older brother about the exotic interior of Africa. So she bought a one-way ticket to Kenya, and for the next couple of years she walked through the East African bush, on her own with no plan or itinerary, sleeping out or in the compound of some village, with only a curved hunting knife for protection.

Two weeks after returning to London, with no idea where her life would take her next, she was invited to a cocktail party by some old friends. A man with a German accent began asking her about her travels. When he heard her story, he was silent for a moment.

"I wonder if you would like to come to lunch tomorrow with my wife and me."

He gave her his card and left. "E. F. Schumacher," it said. Schumacher was the father of the emerging ecology movement, a proponent of using appropriate technology in developing countries, and the author of the international bestseller at that time *Small Is Beautiful*.

The next day he and his wife explained that their organization had been planning to start London's first African Art Gallery, which would also be the first ethnic gallery in which all profits would go to the local artists and craftspeople.

"We think you are the perfect person to run it," they said. "You have just the right combination of design experience and knowledge of Africa."

In months Braeda was on the front page of the *London Times*, dressed in a tribal outfit that the Masai had made especially for her. Over the next five years the gallery would become a major landmark, a cultural crossroads, and a showcase for African culture. Every month Braeda would return to Kenya to give the proceeds to the local people and to order more work.

Even Woody Allen couldn't have made up that story. These kinds of emergent patterns don't make sense, and they nearly always show up as a surprise, seemingly out of left field. However they turn out, we feel that they carry a kind of rightness, that they had to happen because they did. They fit into the intelligence of our life's pattern, and they are keys to our deeper meaning and purpose. What moments like this need from us above all is trust — trust in the mysterious intelligence of our own life rather than the conscious mind's anxious need to control outcomes. Braeda had that trust. She followed the thread of her deeper life's purpose into Africa and back again, without even knowing what the outcome would be. In following that thread she exemplified the belonging, the intrinsic meaning, that is always available to us, the union with the moment we are living now and the willingness to go where it beckons.

Virginia Woolf came to this realization of intrinsic meaning when she was very young:

If life has a base that it stands upon...then my bowl without a doubt stands upon this memory. It is of lying half asleep, half awake, in bed in the nursery of

St. Ives. It is of hearing the waves...breaking, one, two, one, two, behind a yellow blind. It is of hearing the blind draw its little acorn across the floor as the wind blew the blind out. It is of lying and hearing... and feeling, it is almost impossible that I should be here.

The base that Woolf's life stood on was the sheer feeling of existence. It wasn't about this or that function or direction but about simply the raw fact of being, in which the need for complicated explanations falls away. She felt intensely alive not because of anything she was doing, but because *she experienced herself as being — being aware of herself.*

The only time you can be consciously present to your life is now, in this moment, no matter what you are doing or not doing — washing dishes, writing a book, walking the dog, staring into space. If you are fully immersed in the present, aware of the life streaming through your body, then life is so meaningful that the question of meaning and purpose doesn't even arise. The question of belonging doesn't arise. This moment we are living now becomes inherently meaningful for no other reason than that it is being fully lived.

If we human beings have any ultimate purpose, surely

it must be this: to let go of our resistance to life as it is showing up now, now in this very moment, whatever it looks like, rosy or dark. I hum, I sweat, I laugh, I cry, I sing myself home. The moment we are living, whatever it looks like, becomes our purpose made manifest. This is what the sage Krishnamurti meant when he said, "This is my secret: I don't mind what happens."

However, I *do* mind what happens some of the time! Sometimes I mind when the waiter doesn't take my order as quickly as I'd like. I do not rest in a loving awareness of my existence all the time; the clouds do not always pass freely through the sky of my mind.

So while it's true that I struggle much less now with what happens, my fallible sense of self can still be led astray by my thoughts and feelings and desires and longings. And yet even that is okay. I have learned to be kind to myself, to know that I am human because fallibility goes along with being human. Like Jena Lee Nardella, I find myself less and less interested in trying to fix myself or the world and more and more drawn to loving this sorrow, that joy, this lack of purpose, that elation. After all, we are all in this leaky old boat together, going who knows where.

Every moment of forgetting is another opportunity to remember what deep down inside, beyond all ideas of meaning and purpose, I know with a knowing that is not of the mind: that I am the aware, loving presence that is always here. To remember this, especially in the midst of my daily doings, is what I am here for. Everything else will follow.

DROPPING THE STRUGGLE
FOR LOVE

From "Love after Love"

The time will come
When, with elation,
You will greet yourself arriving
At your own door, in your own mirror,
And each will smile at the other's welcome,

And say, Sit here, Eat....

Sit. Feast on your life.

— DEREK WALCOTT

THIS MORNING I WOKE EARLY and felt the tenderness of being alone, the bittersweetness of it. I wondered what the day would bring, a wide-open day that let me sense my own wide-open and tenuous life, and I walked out into the living room and everything, everything was pouring with life, yes, I can say it, brimming with love — the red sofa, the chairs with their pattern of roses, the prints of Rothko, the embroidered tree of life from Iran, even the coffee table with its scattering of books: everything was alive with beauty and the presence of being. I knew then that seeing the world through these eyes, I could never be alone and that I belonged on this earth as surely as an oak tree or a gazelle.

My heart spilled open and the world came alive, and all for no reason. By grace rather than by any effort of my own, the tenderness inside became present without apology or shame, and for a moment or more I was undefended. The undefended heart carries the fragrance of love and bestows a kindness on ourselves and the world.

Being transparent in this way in the presence of another

also happens because it happens — by grace. I recently met an old friend, Athena, whom I had not run into for a couple of years. We had finally managed to arrange a lunch date and were sitting across from each other in a café in San Francisco. "Let me tell you my news," she said. An attractive professional woman in her early fifties, Athena had been in a few relationships since her divorce twenty years earlier, but nothing had felt right. There was always something missing. So she spent most of those years on her own. At different times she had struggled with the fact of being single and had found it difficult to understand why she had not attracted the right partner into her life for such a long time. She had done all the usual things — online dating, meeting friends of friends, going places where people with similar interests would be — but nothing seemed to amount to anything. It was a puzzle, both to her and to her friends. Eventually, she gave up trying and contented herself with the life that she had, which would have been more than fulfilling for most people. But then, she told me across the table, Simin, a young Afghan woman who had become like a daughter to her, reminded her of a promise she had made the previous Christmas.

"Athena, you promised me you would have a boyfriend by this Christmas," Simin had told Athena over breakfast.

"Christmas will be here very soon. I have a strong feeling that this is the year you will find the right man. I know you are happy as you are, but will you do something for me? Please, just for me, try going on Match.com for a couple of weeks. You know, lots of people meet their beloved that way. You just never know what might happen."

"I had gone on Match some years ago and sworn to myself I would never try online dating again," Athena told me. "It felt like a market, so impersonal. But Simin was so insistent that I agreed to try it for just a week, for her sake. I procrastinated for a few months, but after another call from Simin in which she wanted to know my progress, I connected online with this man who lived locally, and we agreed to meet in the bar of a hotel near the waterfront.

"I arrived a few minutes early and the place was crowded with Google employees attending some sort of conference. There was nowhere to sit at the bar, so I came back into the lobby, where there were plenty of seats, and exchanged a smile with a man who was sitting there on his own. I don't know why, but I walked back and asked if the seat by him was vacant. He nodded. As I was sitting down he said, 'You have such a beautiful, open face.'

"It was a spontaneous and genuine comment, and it caught me off guard. (Later, he told me he felt so open it was scary.) I felt warmed by it, and I thanked him. When I was settled he asked what I was there for.

"I paused for a second. What have I got to lose, I thought, in being completely honest with a total stranger. 'I have a Match.com date,' I said. 'I have not met him before, but I don't think he's arrived yet. His name is Jack.'

"'Oh! Are you nervous?' he asked. 'I would be so anxious if I were in your shoes.'

"Within minutes we were talking like the best of friends. His name was Rocco Capobianco. He was as good-looking as his name sounded, and he had an edgy, hip style that I loved. He was in town to give a speech at a tech conference. Despite his name he'd never been to Italy and had always wanted to go. Italy is my favorite country, and I go there whenever I can to learn the language and take cooking classes. Rocco told me he had always wanted to take an Italian cooking class.

"He looked at his watch. 'Hey, it's 6:00 PM,' he said. 'I'll help you look out for Jack. By the way, I love your boots!'

"'Thanks! This is my first-date outfit. What do you think?'

"'You look amazing,' he said. 'Jack will think he hit the jackpot.'

"Only later did I realize the unintended irony of that exchange. In moments we were laughing at the situation, he pointing to someone, me shaking my head, then looking out for the next likely fit to the photo. Fifteen or twenty minutes went by, and in that time we had the easiest conversation — you know, the kind that happens when the chemistry is there and you are on each other's wavelengths.

"I went to look in the bar, but Jack wasn't there. When I sat down again Rocco looked at me and said, 'Look, I know this is weird because you are here waiting for a date, but will you have dinner with me tomorrow night?'

"'Of course, I'd be delighted! I'll phone you now so you will have my number.'

"Rocco looked up from his phone and then nodded in the direction of a man who was walking toward us, with a benignly confused expression on his face.

"'I think that's Jack,' he murmured.

"Flustered and embarrassed, I shot up from my chair, and without even saying good-bye, I went over to Jack and accompanied him into the bar. In half an hour it was evident that he was not someone I would meet again. On my way home I texted Rocco and apologized for not saying good-bye; I had felt so awkward I hadn't known what to do.

"He replied, saying, 'I saw your awkwardness, and you're perfect. Are you still free for dinner tomorrow?'

"That evening was the most delightful I had ever known. It was like meeting a long-lost friend — except it was clear that he was going to be far more than a friend. Our tastes and approach to life were uncannily similar, but it was more than that, more than I can say. A year later we are building a house together."

The two of them let themselves be borne on the wings of fate without even knowing it was happening — a classic example of the erratic principle, or chaos theory, at work. Neither one was trying to make something happen. Neither had sat down with any expectation of saying a word to the other, never mind with any intention of a romance. It was one of those serendipitous moments that have their own rhyme and reason, their own mysterious intelligence.

It all sounds so easy, a dream of a meeting. And yet Athena had been working away inside for years in the way that Rilke implies:

Those who want to have a deep love in their lives must collect and save for it, and gather honey.

Through her own challenging experiences of both love and solitude, she had come to know that love is first and foremost an inside job — not in the sense of trying to love herself with positive affirmations but rather in becoming intimate with her own experience, with allowing herself to be transparent to herself and others rather than protecting her heart for fear of being known too well and then rejected.

She was also engaged in a creative and fulfilling life that she loved. As an individual ripens, *becomes something in herself*, as Rilke puts it, there is less need to find someone else to fill the missing gap. Athena wasn't averse to an intimate relationship; on the contrary, she knew that she wanted one, but she didn't *need* it. All this, I believe, along with her willingness to show up without disguise, contributed to the ease of her encounter with Rocco — who also happened to be *so open it was scary*.

⌒

Yet love between two people is indeed a great work, and that work is often not easy. It is not easy under any circumstance to stay awake to our self-deceptions and unconscious expectations, even less so when it involves someone else who is bound to have misperceptions of his or her own.

So inevitably struggle happens, both inside us and between us. We struggle to find the "right" person, or we launch a campaign, covert or otherwise, to change the person we are with. Yet struggle is not the same as work. Struggle needs us to hold to a position. It needs us to be right and the other to be wrong. Relationship work, on the other hand, needs us to engage in an honest and humble exploration of our vulnerabilities and those of our partner. Struggle tightens our defenses; work can loosen them.

We struggle internally, too — with our beliefs and positions and fears. Why am I not in a relationship? What can I do to call in the One? In the words of the Clash song, "Should I stay or should I go?" Do I want to take on the challenges of being alone or those of engaging in an intimate relationship? How can I honor my needs both for independence and for intimacy?

I am as much a fool in love as anyone, but I have learned that as soon as we stop looking for answers in the self-talk in our head, as soon as we rest back from any position at all, we soften. Then we have enough presence of mind to bring our attention away from the debate and down into our heart, down into our physical presence. Then our body can speak to us. The more we place our attention there, the more a spacious silence can rise in our heart, and miracle of miracles, we may begin to feel the love that is always present, the love that we did not make or decide on, the love that both includes and transcends ourselves and our partner. In that moment, we no longer need to look for love outside, from another person or people; we ourselves are that love.

Stillness, equanimity, love — it seems paradoxical that we can experience these qualities when we step back, disengage, and detach from our thoughts and feelings. But this form of detachment is not a closing off or a disassociation from our experience. It is a deepening of it. The poet Czesław Miłosz, in his poem "Love," says:

Love means to learn to look at yourself
The way one looks at distant things
For you are only one thing among many.
And whoever sees that way heals his heart...
A bird and a tree say to him: Friend.

Perspective, or detachment, heals the heart because it frees us from the illness of self-absorption. It's no longer all about us. It allows us to see that the other has needs, too; that his point of view is as valid to him as ours is to us. We see things in context, as part of a larger picture. If we can look at ourselves this way, we may see that we are "only one thing among many."

When my only son was a child, I was strongly attached to not being woken early, which is still the case. I was also very attached to my morning meditation practice. So when my son would wake up I made it clear that he needed to slip into the family room and stay there, playing on his own until after I had finished my meditation. The obvious — that he was alone and probably lonely — seemed to pass me right by. My habits were more important to me than my son feeling loved. Occasionally I would leap up out of meditation and call to him to be quiet, the irony almost completely lost on me. That was self-absorption, and it wasn't pretty.

Now, decades later, I soften more around the edges of a reaction and stay present, in the stillness that is always the background, to whatever emerges. Another name for that stillness is love. Being willing to let go of the thoughts and feelings that prevent me from living fully into the moment is a humbling process, a lifetime's work that has no arrival point. But my world feels a little more loving as a result; I am more generous both to myself and to others.

⌒

Love between two people includes recognizing the stillness in each other, a placeless place of communion beyond all thoughts about union, beyond all feelings of romantic attraction. Of course, affinities of mind and body are a source of delight and nourishment, and they naturally play their part in bringing two people together, but this communion in the knowing heart is the axis for true love. It can happen in a moment with a passing stranger; it can be the foundation of a lifetime's partnership.

This depth of love asks us to be willing to rest back in a field of trust —not that a particular outcome will follow but in the underlying and ever-present quality of a truly open mind. It is only in the territory of the heart, of love, that trust makes sense.

I am not always in that spacious presence, and when thoughts and feelings take me away I am called to remember that the source of love hasn't gone anywhere. It is I who have wandered away and forgotten myself. I forget what the heart knows: that whatever occurs, all is already fundamentally well.

This spacious sense of being, this stillness in the heart of whatever is going on, is the deepest intimacy we can know with another human being. When I know this stillness to be the core of who I am, I may see myself reflected in the heart of another, still center echoing to still center, and we recognize each other in a loving field of awareness beyond all opinions.

Robert Bly summons this love in his wonderful poem

"The Third Body," in which a man and a woman sit near each other in timeless ease, with no need to speak or not speak, where any gesture floats effortlessly in the spacious air.

> They obey a third body that they share in common.
> They have promised to love that body.
> Age may come, parting may come, death will come.
> A man and a woman sit near each other.

The third body they share is the aware presence that lives and breathes all things. It is love itself. They have surrendered to that love in this moment, given it their full and unconditional trust. The old marriage vows in the Book of Common Prayer speak of honoring and cherishing your beloved. This couple lives those vows without any effort or forethought. When you honor someone you hold her in deep regard. When you cherish her you value her; your heart goes out to her. You want what is best for her, regardless of what it might mean for you.

How does it feel to be in the warmth of a loving regard? Like a plant might feel as it turns toward the sun. We want to be close to the other, touch him, make love with her, maybe, or simply hold his hand. The heart door springs open, and our self-concern dissolves like mist in the morning light. You have probably known this at times in your life, as I have in mine. And perhaps like me you forget. The world presses in, *is too much with us*, as Wordsworth put it, and a longing arises for something we have no name for.

That longing may take the form of desire for another human being, and yet often it becomes a longing for what some call *God*. Most of us have known that longing and the feeling of absence it emerges from. It is prior to religion; it is fundamental to the human experience. It points to what and who we already are. You cannot long for something you do not know, even if you have no name for it.

Rumi, great love poet that he was, urges us, in "Love Dogs," to follow our longing back to its source in the chest, back to the sensation of heartbreak, sorrow, and loss. What a paradox: there in the broken heart is the place of union.

> "This longing you express
> is the return message."
> The grief you cry out from
> draws you to union.
>
> (TRANSLATED BY COLEMAN BARKS)

We are the ones we are looking for. We are the beloved. Derek Walcott sings this truth into high art in his magnificent poem "Love after Love," an excerpt from which is at the beginning of this chapter. When we know this, even for a moment, we see the beloved everywhere. Then all semblance of struggle is forgotten. It's not only the likes of Rumi who knew moments like this. It's a universal human experience that usually goes unrecorded. But Patrick Houck is one person who wrote his experience into a poem.

Patrick was a student in my writing group. He came to our group one evening several months before he died suddenly, in 2015, and read his latest poem. After he had read it, no one spoke for several minutes. I can only say that I knew for certain that every word was true. The mystical love union happened for him at the garden gate on his way to work:

> Eight-year-old Julia is my neighbor,
> we met three weeks ago
> when she asked if she could pet my dog.
> Kneeling, she gently took Zoe's soft and furry ears
> into her hands, like they were precious jewels.
> She brought the entire world down with her,
> in a pure and tender moment.

She stood, thanked me, and walked away.
That day, I felt the
immensity of her heart.

Today at my closed gate, I'm leaving for work,
my heart like a clenched fist.
Julia stands on the other side, ready for school,
looking right into me,
all snug in her quilted pink coat,
her clear eyes free of the future.

She holds me in her gaze
and I take the first breath of the day.
I grow nervous as the one who thinks he knows himself.
She continues to look into me,
a transparent sincerity.
And I, so vulnerable to this beauty and love
so afraid of losing control,
of being helpless before someone so young,
before anyone.
Yet the love softens that, too.

From the inside out,
my whole body opening wide,
gentleness pouring over everything,
bringing down the inner scaffold,

thought falling away, insignificant,
incapable of knowing such immensity.

Then all the way down my heart is breaking, down into
    a vast, infinite love
where we both are ageless, without concern, sacred.

I see reality shining fully…in Julia, in this moment,
    everywhere.
Only what sees is not just me,
what's seeing is also looking from everywhere.
We are in the forever ancient.

She raises her hand, a greeting
and a good-bye.
I raise mine; she turns and walks off to school.

Later, as I head down a new street,
looking at the freshness of things,
I am shaking.
Shaking with the certainty
that I have just seen god.

A realization such as this poem embodies — that *what's
seeing is also looking from everywhere* — is the deepest intimacy we can know, beyond even the soulful intimacy of

the couple in Bly's poem. It is an intimacy not with anyone in particular, but with all things, with life itself as it lives through us and through everything. It reaches right down into our bones — *my whole body opening wide...all the way down my heart is breaking* — and joins us not only to the beauty but also to the great suffering of this living world.

It is the ultimate knowing that there is in the deep heart no separation, that we are and always have been in an inherent condition of belonging, not in our smaller identity but in our greater identity with life itself as it lives us. You can't make such a realization happen. You can't practice for it. You certainly can't struggle to attain it. But like Patrick Houck, you can till your inner ground over a lifetime and be open without even knowing it to the workings of grace.

DROPPING THE STRUGGLE WITH TIME

I Am Not I

I am not I.
I am this one
walking beside me whom I do not see,
whom at times I manage to visit,
and whom at other times I forget;
who remains calm and silent while I talk,
and forgives, gently, when I hate,
who walks where I am not,
who will remain standing when I die.

— JUAN RAMÓN JIMÉNEZ,
translated by Robert Bly

I WAS SITTING IN THE SHADE of the pipal tree in the courtyard to the entrance of Ramana Maharshi's cave, where,
before he died in 1950, the great sage lived for eighteen
years on the slopes of Mt. Arunachala in Tamil Nadu,
India. The courtyard was filled, mostly with middle-class
Indian women swathed in bright colors, all of them gazing at a slight, middle-aged man in simple white. The only
sound was the wind in the tree and the faint hum of traffic
far below.

Years before, Nanagaru had been a simple farmer.
One night he was awoken by a powerful dream image of
a man's face, a man with exceptionally soft and compassionate eyes. The next morning he opened the newspaper
and there was a photograph of the man he had seen in the
night. It was Ramana Maharshi. Nanagaru found out where
Ramana's ashram was, and although the saint had died
years earlier, Nanagaru made his way as soon as he could
to Tiruvannamalai, the town at the foot of Mt. Arunachala.
On his first morning there, between sleeping and waking,
he — as he put it to me — felt his mind falling once and for

all into his heart. From then on he was a changed man. He felt himself to be living by a force other than his personality. People began to gather about him, and his name spread quickly throughout southern India.

It was late afternoon and the courtyard was warm, even in the shade of the pipal tree. Nanagaru had been sitting in silence along with everyone else. Then he turned and gestured to me.

"Mr. Roger thinks he is going away to England tomorrow on a plane. But he is not going anywhere. He never goes anywhere. He never moves. His body moves, and his mind moves, but he does not move."

Nanagaru laughed and let out a belch. I was so full of travel plans that day that at first I didn't really catch his meaning. Then with a jolt I remembered a similar encounter a few years earlier, with a man called Poonjaji, another teacher who had been awoken through his connection with Ramana. I had been sitting in his tiny living room in Lucknow. It was 1990.

Poonja was a more imposing presence than Nanagaru, a large man with an even larger presence that filled the room. At that time few people knew him yet, and he had not been easy to track down. When my partner at the time, Chloe, and I were ushered into their house by his wife, he motioned for us to sit down and, pulling out a train timetable, asked which train we had taken to arrive in Lucknow. Then he gossiped for fifteen minutes or so about the best and worst trains to Lucknow, asking the other two people present which trains they had arrived on. Then he turned to me suddenly and said, "What can I do for you, Mr. Roger?" (Everyone in India seemed to want to call me Mr. Roger.)

I faltered.

"I find it difficult to reconcile nondualism with my own experience of devotion and love," I said at last. "If there is only one reality, how are we to account for the existence of love, since love requires a relationship?"

Poonja roared with laughter — I seemed regularly to evoke this response from teachers in India. "Now who is asking the question?" he replied. "Is it the question of a philosopher or a lover? Either way you are missing the point. What is the point? *You* are the point. Who are you? That is where you will find your answer. Tell me, Mr. Roger, who is it that has come to India in the disguise of this body I see before me? If you can speak as that, you will know all about love."

"I suppose I can only say I don't know who I am. I am beyond my own thoughts and words."

"But who is saying this to me at this very moment?

What is the source of these words and this talk about love?"

I sat there in silence. Poonja smiled. "When I first went to see Ramana," he said, taking the heat off me, "I asked him to grant me the vision of Lord Krishna. At that time I was mad with love for Krishna. I had been a lover of his form since childhood, and had always longed for the sight of his presence. 'Go and meditate on Arunachala Mountain,' Ramana said to me. So I did, and sure enough, Krishna came to me in person. He was really there, in front of me, and I played with him like a child. When I returned to Ramana and told him about my vision, he asked me, 'Where is your Krishna now?' 'He is not here now,' I replied. 'Then rest alone with that which never comes and never goes away,' said Ramana. In that moment I knew the unchanging truth of my own existence, and who I thought I was died forever."

Both Poonja and Nanagaru were pointing me to the timeless dimension beyond the mind. They wanted me to see that I was literally not who I thought I was, that my true identity was the silent, aware presence beyond thought, beyond space and time. Clearly I had forgotten the insight I had glimpsed with Poonja by the time I was sitting with Nanagaru. It took a very unspiritual encounter with two

Iranian intelligence officials many years later for me to know in a less fleeting way what for the two Indians was as obvious as the hands in front of their faces.

Yet even at the time, it seemed to me that Poonja's preoccupation with the railway timetable was pointing to a second teaching. Without stating it, he was making the point that although our deeper nature is timeless, clock time and attention to the details of ordinary life are nevertheless crucial, too. Our world couldn't run as it is without the construction of time — even if time is no more than a brilliant creation of the human mind.

We have run — and been all too easily run by— time since the introduction of railway time in England in the early nineteenth century. For me, Poonja was pointing to the big question of how to live in both worlds concurrently: the timeless dimension and clock time. In Christian terms, it's what Jesus meant by being in the world but not of it. This is the message in the poem by Jiménez above.

Standardized time spread from England across the globe with the spread of the railways. And everything changed. The timeless procession of the seasons, of agricultural time, gave way to the hours and minutes and seconds of clock time. People began to have to clock in to work. Today, every minute counts.

Time is money, as they say. As a culture, we hate the notion of wasting time, of losing time, and we often find ourselves running out of time, fighting against the clock. Time is associated with being productive, with getting things done in good time. In America people feel guilty for taking a vacation. Doing nothing is almost sinful. But what really *is* a waste of time? The only time we objectively have is this moment we are living now. What determines whether or not it is wasted? The poet James Wright raises that question in his poem "Lying in a Hammock at William Duffy's Farm in Pine Island, Minnesota." He is lying in a hammock, his eyes on a bronze butterfly on the tree trunk, his ears aware of the cowbells in *the distances of the afternoon.*

A chicken hawk floats over, looking for home.
I have wasted my life.

Lying in a hammock is the perfect metaphor for the willingness to do nothing, nothing at all. To forgo all duties and responsibilities, to lie back and let go of the current struggle. Perhaps the reason we allow ourselves so little of this sort of luxury is that we are afraid we and our lives will slip through our fingers, that without the rod so many of us have made for our backs, we would turn into jelly, devoid of all will..Even worse, we would cease to exist if we weren't doing something useful.

After all, the psychological self is rooted in time. It needs to feel it is on a journey, that it is getting somewhere — anywhere. The journey is what provides it with a feeling of existence and continuity. If it weren't going somewhere it would be forced to feel the fear of the present moment, the fear of not existing, of the void beneath its feet. Our individual journey is reinforced by the cultural norm. Our culture is so fixated on the necessity of *doing* that if we are idle for a while we are very likely to think we are wasting our time and our lives. Everyone wants to "have a life" and "get a life," and that usually means throwing ourselves into some gainful activity that will show a tangible result. It certainly doesn't mean lazing around in a hammock. That is for losers or sick people.

This is not the way James Wright sees it. Having a life, for him, meant feeling the aliveness and clarity and ease that he experienced while lying in the hammock that day. His poem shows how aware and in touch he was with his present experience. It didn't mean that he wanted to lie in a hammock all day. It meant that the peace, the presence, he felt there was the closest he knew to a life well and fully lived — a life, then, determined less by its productivity than by the quality of experience known moment by moment. He became aware in that hammock of how few moments like this he had allowed himself. A wasted life, he realized, is one that is not suffused with moments of pure, aware presence.

That poem was written before the Internet existed. Lying without distraction in a hammock, or doing its equivalent, is more challenging now. When did you last lie on your deck or your sofa without your phone? I am as susceptible to distraction as anyone. I rarely look at emails while writing, but I did a few minutes ago. And serendipity! There was an email from Rick Hanson, the author of *Hardwiring Happiness.* It was his newsletter; the newsletter's heading was "Drop the Load." In it Rick says, "Getting stuff done sometimes seems like the secular religion of the developed world, especially in America, where we routinely make sacrifices at the altar of doingness. I'm this way myself: my main compulsion/addiction is crossing off items on my To Do list."

Yet it's not the to-do list that's the problem. It is, as Rick implies, our compulsive addiction to getting through it. It's not what we do that determines the quality of our experience so much as the way we do it. Obsessive activity has our attention fixed on an ever-receding future. We rush through something because we imagine we will feel good when we have finished. But we don't, because there is always something else to do. The to-do list is never ending. It keeps us running away from the gap, the space of the present moment. And that is the whole point — the psychological self, the ego, needs to feel it is getting somewhere, so the goalposts continually have to be pushed further into the future.

A century and a half ago, Kierkegaard argued that this impulse to escape the present by keeping ourselves busy is our greatest source of unhappiness. We jump on the hamster wheel of activity early in life. As the thinking self develops, we are less and less able to tolerate periods of boredom, moments or times when nothing is happening, and we don't know what to do with ourselves. In other words, when nothing is happening, we feel that *we* are not happening.

Can we resist the desire to take the phone along with us on our walk? Can we sit quietly for half an hour without doing anything? The feeling of our own presence is the richest gift we can offer ourselves. Those "empty" moments — in the traffic jam, the checkout line, the airport lounge — can sometimes offer us a further gift. If we don't run from them, if we rest in them and let them take us where they will, we may find that they connect us to a deeper well, a source of creative ideas and inspirations that erupts from behind the conscious mind.

Writers know this well. A large part of my writing time is spent lying on the sofa looking out of the window, walking around the room, or perhaps going for a walk in the woods outside. You can only stare at the blank screen for so long. Sometimes the gates open and the words come pouring onto the screen. At other times it is best to do nothing, to look the other way, so to speak. "I only went out for a walk," John Muir said, "and finally concluded to stay out till sundown, for going out, I found, was really going in."

Our greatest art, the most enduring ideas of philosophy, the spark for every technological breakthrough — originated in moments of reflective contemplation, of absolute presence within the universe of one's own mind and absolute attentiveness to life outside it, be it Galileo inventing the modern clock after watching a pendulum swing in a cathedral or Oliver Sacks having seminal insights into the power of music on the human mind while hiking in a Norwegian fjord.

Reflective contemplation is the original meaning of the word *leisure*. The Greek term came into the Latin as *scola*, from which we get the word *school*. A school, or university, was originally intended as a place of leisure, of contemplative activity, not as a place that prepared you for work. Leisure, in the High Middle Ages and into the Renaissance, meant the ability to reflect on human existence through the study of the arts, music, and philosophy. It is a condition of soul, not to be confused with idleness, which is a slackness of spirit. James Wright was at leisure in his hammock; he wasn't being idle.

The Benedictine monk David Steindl-Rast, in his *Essential Writings*, points out that leisure need not be separate from work itself, that time and the timeless can coexist. To work in a leisurely way is the highest expression of work. "Leisure...is not the privilege of those who can afford to take time; it is the virtue of those who give to everything they do the time it deserves to take."

Obsessive doing — rushing through an activity to get it over with — kills time. Leisurely activity makes time come alive because it connects us to the timeless. Artists of all kinds know this. Chefs know this. I am not a chef by any stretch of the imagination, but I love cooking and generally make up recipes as I go along. But when my hands are peeling the sprouts or washing the lettuce or cutting the salmon, my enjoyment comes not from the anticipated dish but from the trickle of water through my fingers, the smell of the sea from the salmon, the whir of the spinner as I dry the lettuce. Leisure fosters not only pleasure but enjoyment, and enjoyment happens when we are fully immersed in our experience, at the intersection of doing and being.

Rushing is not as enjoyable. We are always at least a step ahead of ourselves and forever straining to catch up. Rushing stops up the gaps in consciousness through which the creative muse can speak. It exhausts not only our physical but also our psychic energy. Over time it will exhaust our spirit, especially when we tell ourselves that these are things we *must* do, *should* do, or *have* to do. Then we lose all sense of agency and choice.

Obsessive doing happens not only externally but also in our minds, which are endlessly churning over thoughts and rerunning emotions. Outwardly, we may be doing no more than staring out the window or lying in a hammock, but inwardly we can be totally lost in the past or future. Then we are obscuring the present moment, which is the doorway to our own silent, aware presence, our deepest source of fulfillment and aliveness.

We struggle with the past when we won't let it go,

when we gnaw at it like a dog with a bone, endlessly chewing over something whose juice has long ago been sucked dry. We know we are struggling with the past when the same scenarios rise up in our minds over and over, without resolution. Does this mean we should never have thoughts of the past? Of course not; and anyway, that would be impossible. The mind churns out thoughts of the past and the future like a spaghetti machine. It's part of its job. The past gives us the security of a journey, the continuum of a story, and we all need a story as long as we live. The difference lies in how lightly or tightly we hold on to that story.

It's not the past that is the problem; it is the way we hang on to it, repeat it, regurgitate it, mostly in order to give ourselves a false sense of substance and identity. The problem arises when our stories of the past consume our attention in the present and prevent us from being fully available to the life we are living now. The signs of that malady are anxiety, regret, and the reliving of old thoughts and emotions. The past doesn't have to take us over like that. If we maintain our attention in the present moment; if we remember to rest back into the stillness that is always here, then the past can serve a useful purpose right now as a memory library that we can use as a resource when necessary.

Neither is the future a problem unless our plans and

fantasies so swamp our present experience that we are living in a dreamland rather than in the life we actually have. Surely one of the greatest gifts of the human mind is its capacity for forward thinking. The great projects of civilization were all the result of imagining some future scenario and working toward it in the present. No business would ever succeed without a business plan. No contract would be good for more than the day it was signed on.

The future becomes a problem only when our need for security compels us to worry and make up stories about what might happen or could happen. We've all gotten to the end of a long-anticipated meal only to realize that we have not been conscious of the taste of a single mouthful because we were fretting over some meeting later in the day.

That doesn't mean we stop having future plans. It means we recognize we are asking too much of those future plans. Future events may cause a spike in our oxytocin levels for an hour or day or two, but they will never fulfill the sense of lack that we feel now. The sense of lack exists because we are not experiencing the only fulfillment that is truly available to us, which is the presence of this moment. We will never experience it if we are always running ahead of ourselves into the future or ruminating over the past.

The great work of being human is to live in the worlds of stillness and movement, time and timelessness, at one and the same time. You don't have to *get* to silence, openness, awareness; in fact, you can't. You only have to recognize that the stillness at the center of time is already here. It's a direct experience, not a journey. Dropping the struggle with time isn't something you do; it's a spontaneous relaxation, a falling backward into what is already present. When we know the stillness at our core as a lived experience in the everyday, we breathe more easily, we go about our days differently. To be still and still moving is to know the end of time, even as the clock is ticking.

DROPPING THE STRUGGLE WITH CHANGE

Our revels now are ended. These, our actors,
As I foretold you, were all spirits, and
Are melted into air, into thin air.
And, like the baseless fabric of this vision,
The cloud-capp'd towers, the gorgeous palaces,
The solemn temples, the great globe itself,
Yea, all which it inherit, shall dissolve,
And, like this insubstantial pageant faded,
Leave not a rack behind. We are such stuff
As dreams are made on; and our little life
Is rounded with a sleep.

— SHAKESPEARE, *THE TEMPEST*, ACT 4, SCENE I

WHEN YOU READ THESE LINES from *The Tempest* today, you might take *the great globe itself* to mean the world as we know it, and you would be right, but only partly. The Globe was also the name of Shakespeare's theater in London on the south bank of the Thames, the theater that he and his company had worked so furiously to make a success since its first performance in 1599. *The Tempest* was performed there for the first time in November 1611. Just eighteen months after those lines from *The Tempest* had first echoed around the Globe, the theater was razed by fire.

Shakespeare's lines were prescient, but all his plays reveal an intimate awareness of the transience of all life, all things, and all people. His own son, Hamnet, died of the Black Death, or bubonic plague, in 1596, and it's no coincidence that *Hamlet*, by far his most introspective and psychological play, was written just a year or two later. His seven-year-old sister, Anne, died when he was fourteen. In his era one in three children died before the age of ten. Death was always in plain view, unlike today, when it is airbrushed away.

The world changed quickly then, just as it does now. In Shakespeare's lifetime England threw off a thousand years of Catholic belief and ritual, and Catholics suddenly became the enemies of the state. Shakespeare's family of origin, always deeply Catholic, was not above suspicion. England became a police state, with informers on every corner. Then Mary Queen of Scots came to the throne, and for five years the Catholics had a reprieve while it became the Protestants' turn to be burned at the stake. When Mary died, everything changed again, and England returned to being Protestant. These were intensely traumatic culture shocks that in just a few years shook the worldview of the general population to its very foundations.

Shakespeare did not just endure those shocks; he absorbed them and turned them into art, into the passion and hard-won wisdom for which his plays are revered. Shakespeare knew, not from any religious or philosophical text, but in his bones that this world and everything in it — everything and everyone that we hold dear — is already leaving, even now, as you read these words on the page. These words themselves are no more than tenuous and shifting placeholders for the thoughts of this moment that are already being replaced by fresh thoughts, like the appearing and disappearing words written with a trick pen on the same sheet of white paper.

Not only is everything that our senses reveal to us of the outer world a constantly shifting kaleidoscope, forever ungraspable; so too is our inner world of thoughts, feelings, and sensations, all of which are constantly changing, without any unified identity holding them together. Shakespeare goes even further in his line *We are such stuff as dreams are made on.* Who we take ourselves to be is no more than a dream, he says. There is no Roger sitting somewhere behind the eyes thinking those thoughts, feeling those feelings, and generally steering the ship of his life. None of what we take ourselves to be is any more substantial than a passing dream image, which will vanish from view when the dream ends in death.

This may seem more familiar to us today as a Buddhist philosophy, but Shakespeare was saying the same thing in the seventeenth century. No tradition or people has a patent on the truth. People in all times and places have recognized the dreamlike nature of what we take to be our solid identity. David Hume, one of the founding fathers of the Enlightenment, born almost a hundred years after Shakespeare died, said, "When I enter most intimately into what

I call *myself*, I always stumble on some particular perception or other, of heat or cold, light or shade, love or hatred, pain or pleasure. I never can catch *myself* at any time without a perception, and never can observe anything but the perception."

Change itself is the one certainty we can be absolutely sure of. You might say this is obvious. We all know this already. Except that we don't, or at least we don't often act as if we do, when change arrives on our doorstep. We may have lived for years as the lead character in a story that has enabled us to feel secure in our job, in our family relationships, in our place in the world. Or we may have lived for decades secure in the story of our suffering, the injustice done to us, the bad hand we were given.

Either way, our belief in the story is what creates some sense of a solid identity, which in turn gives us the illusion of security. But then the house of cards can fall at any time, as we also know from our experience, which is why, deep down, however rosy our picture may seem, a constant vein of subliminal anxiety about what might happen next is likely to be running through us.

Our life is already, even now, slipping through our

fingers. So given that nothing we are familiar with, including ourselves, is going to last, how can we live another day without breaking out into a cold sweat?

We can bow to whatever passes across our landscape. We can trust the inscrutable intelligence of the life that is living us, as it is showing up for us, in this very moment. If it is sorrow, let us make friends with sorrow. Let us not drown but swim in the waters of sorrow. Naomi Shihab Nye, in her wonderful poem "Kindness," says that if you are ever to know what kindness really is,

You must lose things,
feel the future dissolve in a moment
like salt in a weakened broth.

Why does she say this? Because the experience of loss brings us close, not only to someone dear whom we may have lost but to the whole of humanity; for every individual has and always will know loss. Loss breaks the heart open, and when the heart breaks open we become a kindness to ourselves and to the world.

In the great themes of life — love, loss, parting, and death — poetry can surpass scripture in slipping the visceral experience of a deep truth into the bloodstream. It feeds the imagination with shimmering images more than the mind with the letter of the truth. In his *Sonnets to Orpheus*, Rilke urges us:

> Want the change. Be inspired by the flame
> Where everything shines as it disappears.
>
> (translated by anita barrows
and joanna macy)

Exquisite image! Why does he exhort us to want the change? Because change is the way it is. We harbor notions of what is good for us and what is not, and try to organize and strategize accordingly. Yet life does what it does without concern for our preferences, so Rilke is urging us to look beyond the parade of circumstances and events to the fundamental fact of change itself. In wanting the change, we are aligning ourselves with truth, with what is already happening.

We flow rather than self-consciously make our way. In that flow, the sense of who we are and where we are going becomes more malleable and fluid, more responsive to the conditions around us instead of bound by fixed beliefs and agendas. In the flow of change, we forget ourselves, and a deeper remembrance emerges — the remembrance of being always and ever joined to a greater life — not as an elegant concept but as a lived experience in the moment.

So Rilke is urging us to want the change that is happening, to embrace it, whatever it is. If we are in the middle of a divorce, let it be that. If we have lost our job, let it be that, and if we are dying, may it be so. Of course it's not easy. Nobody willingly allows herself to be dismembered, torn apart, crushed like a grape between the fingers. The ego will never assent to the sacrifice of the story it has so lovingly tended. The impulse must come from something else in us, another organ of awareness, you might say, that knows somehow, however much it hurts, however much we may be on the rack — a sacrificial lamb, it may seem to us — that what is happening is true, necessary, inevitable, and ultimately, therefore, good.

Rilke's image of everything shining more brightly as the flame disappears captures with arresting force what so many of us know about loss: how what we are losing — our life, a loved one — becomes all the more precious as we realize it is not here to stay. I had never been ill in my life, and had not been in a hospital until 2012, when it was discovered by chance that I had an aneurysm of the upper aorta, the main artery that ascends from the heart and channels blood around the body. Had I not had open-heart surgery to repair the artery, it likely would have burst and I would have been gone without a good-bye.

After the surgery I started getting weaker and weaker rather than stronger. Belatedly, it was discovered that I had a blood clot in one of my lungs. Then the pericardium — the sac around the heart — began filling with fluid, which was only noticed just as my heart was beginning to have to beat underwater. Surgeons were rushed in from another hospital to drain the fluid. Another half an hour, and I would have been dead.

Lying on that gurney, waiting for the specialist surgeon to arrive, I gazed out at the dear friends, Jennifer Welwood and Palden Alioto, who had brought me in. My mind was still, and I can honestly say I knew nothing but a silent love for my friends and also for the doctors and nurses surrounding me. The love was neither emotional nor conceptual. I can only describe it as utter nonresistance without thought. I did not try to have this response to my situation; it happened. It was a grace in which there was no trace of fear and no thought for what might happen next. There was no next. There was only lying there on that gurney, draped in a blue hospital gown, gazing.

Even before the surgeon drained my pericardium and life energy poured through my body again as if someone had turned on a spigot, I felt grateful. Somehow I knew with an inner knowing that all was truly well, whatever happened. But I am under no illusion that I will experience my next big loss, whatever shape it comes in, in the same way. Perhaps fear will rock my foundations and turn me to stone. I don't know. Each moment, new moment.

What matters is that we allow what happens, whatever it is, that we don't rationalize or spiritualize it away either by minimizing the loss or trying to bypass it with attempts to rise above it. The Greek poet Constantine Cavafy warns Antony and Cleopatra of this in his magnificent poem "The God Abandons Antony." They are losing their beloved city of Alexandria, and Antony is also losing the protection of his tutelary deity, Dionysius, god of wine and song. Cavafy wants us to feel, through Antony, the experience of losing what is most precious to us, without giving any thought to what might happen next:

> Above all, don't fool yourself, don't say
> it was a dream, your ears deceived you:
> don't degrade yourself with empty hopes like these.
>
> (TRANSLATED BY EDMUND KEELEY
> AND PHILIP SHERRARD)

Cavafy urges Antony to *listen with deep emotion* to the reality of what he is losing. *Deep emotion* does not mean acting out; it means being willing to allow the loss into your bloodstream, to let its fire fan out from the heart and find its way into the cells of the body. To listen to the course of your life, to accept it *with deep emotion* instead of trying to bargain with God, your lover, even your enemy — and instead of trying to follow the fashionable idea of creating a reality of one's own choosing — to listen like this is to keep the embers of your true life burning, even in your darkest winter. Cavafy is calling Mark Antony in this way — and by extension, us, the readers — to our essential human dignity.

⌁

The biggest change we are likely to know is when old age, sickness, or death comes knocking at our door, or at the door of someone close to us. This shouldn't be, we think. This can't be. Even though we know conceptually that our life has an end-by date, even though we know that people lose limbs every day, get sick every day, die every day — even so, disbelief is the most common first response to a sudden change in our faculties. It's always a shock when the body or mind we have been so used to as a more or less willing servant decides to go on strike either for a while or for good.

If we are sick or lose a motor skill or some of our memory, does the conventional spiritual wisdom of surrender simply imply that we give up all struggle to live and let nature take its course? Does trusting your life's intelligence mean that we don't take measures to care for ourselves?

In 2014, at the age of eighty-eight, the famous Buddhist teacher Thich Nhat Hanh had a severe stroke that left him largely paralyzed and unable to speak. When Thay, as his students call him, first started physical therapy, he was very engaged and enthusiastic with his therapists and the program they had created for him. "Preparing for Thay's sessions of physical therapy," his disciples wrote in their newsletter, "we could all feel the joyful determination in his body language. We would tell him, 'Thay, let's get ready for physical therapy' and Thay would raise his fist in the air and smile, as if to say 'Let's go!'"

His disciples brought him from his center in France to San Francisco, where he could benefit from the very best of Western, Eastern, conventional, and alternative medical approaches. Thay received acupuncture every day, as well as physical therapy, speech therapy, osteopathy, and neuro-feedback, with the support and oversight of the very best doctors at UCSF.

In their newsletter, his disciples say:

> Every day Thay continues to remind us to enjoy the wonders of life, often pointing at the blue sky and helping us come back to the present moment. Sometimes Thay playfully switches roles with the doctors and therapists, putting a finger on his lips and inviting them to stop. In these moments he often indicates for us to prepare tea so his doctors can have a chance to enjoy a cup of tea in mindfulness. One therapist knelt down by his side, looking out of the window and began to cry silently. She later shared with us that it was perhaps the first time in her life that she had really stopped and appreciated the blue of the sky.

Thich Nhat Hanh is living his own teaching right to the very end. He is eagerly doing all he can to improve his condition. What he has dropped — what, in his case, he never had in the first place — was an investment in any treatment to get the result he might want. His attention is not on some future date when he hopes to be well, or on his prognosis. It rests where it has been all his long life — on each moment as it arises in his consciousness and in the consciousness of those around him. Even in his hospital bed, seriously impaired, he was an inspiration to others to live to the full the only moment that is ever possible, the one that is here now — even if this breath is the last.

There was a moment in the hospital when he managed to utter his first few words. They were, "In, out, happy, thank you." In January of 2016 Thay was able to return to his center in France, where he continues to exemplify his lifetime's teachings.

DROPPING THE STRUGGLE TO KNOW

FROM *THE SECOND BOOK OF THE TAO*

To act without needing a reason,
To sit still without knowing how,
To ride the current of what is —
This is the primal virtue.

— CHUANG-TZU,
translated by Stephen Mitchell

IT'S SATISFYING TO THINK WE KNOW WHO WE ARE, where we are going, and what we are here for. Of course it is. Yet if we are lucky, a time may come when we have the opportunity to exchange all our answers for bewilderment. Every tradition points to this moment. There is a medieval Christian text called *The Cloud of Unknowing*; there is the old Zen exhortation *Only Don't Know*. These are wisdom phrases, expressions of insight, and they point to what is always essentially unknowable, which is the mystery itself, the ungraspable ground from which all our experiences emerge. Another name for that ground is I Am. Who I am can only be experienced. It can only be pointed to by a jaw dropped open, speechless.

In everyday life, as distinct to some dedicated spiritual practice, the awareness that I am can sometimes reveal itself in the gap, the empty space that arises when our mind no longer knows what to do or which way to turn. It emerges when we finally drop the struggle to know, to understand — when we fall back from being a knowledgeable subject and surrender to our utter helplessness before the immensity of life's mystery.

Dante's *Divine Comedy* begins with these immortal words:

In the middle of my life I found myself in a dark wood, the right way entirely lost.

It was only after Dante let go of all his bearings and acknowledged he was hopelessly lost that he looked up and saw the light of the sun in the far distance over a mountain. He had no guide or map or set of instructions. Only a wordless knowing, *born out of his helplessness, his unknowing*, showed him that was the direction to follow. The light of the sun was the mirror for the knowing, the sun, which shone inside him.

This kind of knowing, always present in us, does not come from our thinking mind. Being just knows; it doesn't know this or that, but its inherent nature is knowing. Its knowing is nonconceptual, a knowing field, like an endless sky that stretches far beyond its own weather system of thoughts and feelings. And paradoxically, our willingness not to know allows the sky to suddenly clear for us and be free for a while of passing clouds.

In 1998 my life had reached a crossroads, and I had no idea what to do or where to go. All I knew was that I could not go on as I had. All the plans and ideas and strategies I had turned over in my mind for months had led nowhere. I was in Dante's dark wood, with no way out.

Then one morning in early spring, in that open space between sleeping and waking, I knew, but it was a knowing without words. I don't know how or why, I don't know where it came from, but I knew with a visceral certainty, with a warmth that flooded my body, that I was to leave my native country of England and go live in America. Just like that. The thought had never occurred to me before. It wasn't a decision; it was like recognizing something whose time had come. I had known already that everything needed to change, but now it was time to act.

On the one hand, the move to America was a long time coming. I was fifty-three at the time. On the other, it took no time whatsoever. One day, one moment, this kind of knowing just happens. It happens outside ordinary time. It swoops in sideways, and like the swallow, is the harbinger of new things, of a new caste of mind.

I sold my house and my library; my love of twelve years and I parted; I read all my diaries of twenty-five years and then burned them. I got on a plane to California, and have been there, in a new life, ever since. Perhaps this sounds too dramatic, too grand a gesture somehow for the kind of lives that most of us lead — including my own. Yet at the time it didn't seem dramatic at all. It was the only thing to do. I let go of trying to steer my ship with the rudder of my plans and let a new life, one that I had not even thought of, fill my sail.

When we drop the struggle to find our way and surrender to our complete bewilderment, a new quality of knowing, as distinct to knowledge, can emerge. *Knowing* is an active term, a process; *knowledge*, the noun, is static, and resides only in the memory. Google will always direct us to more knowledge than we can ever absorb, but it will never reveal the knowing that co-arises with being — with who we are.

We act most authentically when our actions come directly from this knowing beyond words. Then our actions come from a larger intelligence that somehow allows us to act without acting — that is, spontaneous, embodied action without the sensation of being a separate self trying to exert its will on the world. The liminal world between sleeping and waking is one of the portals through which such silent knowing can burst into consciousness. That was what happened to me that morning in 1998.

Our lives make their traces in the ocean that Rumi speaks of in his poem "Buoyancy":

The sea-journey goes on, and who knows where!

Each of us carves our own wake without any idea of what lies ahead. Yet as Rumi says in that same poem, the ocean doesn't care what patterns we make. That boundless ocean of knowing presence surrounds us in the most tender, accepting embrace, no matter who we are and what we do. What matters, he says in that same poem, is that you *feel the motions of tenderness around you, the buoyancy.* Then *it's a total waking up!*

To wake up is to rest back into the ocean, which is present now, right where we are. To become one with that field of silent knowing, we have only to drop the knower, our familiar self who knows this and that, the one who has a strategy and thinks she can work her way into heaven. In that same poem, Rumi says,

> Love has taken away my practices
> And filled me with poetry.
>
> (TRANSLATED BY COLEMAN BARKS)

He has dropped all his spiritual practices because he sees that there is nothing he can do of his own will. As he floats on the ocean, the only thing that comes out of his mouth is poetry because poetry is inspired utterance, not a teaching. Rumi's poetry arose out of the ocean.

When the idea of a centralized self — what Ramana Maharshi called "the I-thought" — falls away, even for a moment, when we forget ourselves, so to speak, then we see beyond our own name. Whenever we slip behind the name of something — anyone, anything — we stand before an open doorway to Mystery, in which there is no longer any solid boundary between you and me, this and that. The writer Gabriel García Márquez said of his wife, "I know her so well that she is completely and utterly unknown to me." In that unknowing, differences fall away and love arises.

You might ask yourself now: Who is it that is looking out of these eyes and following these words across the page? What is this before you that is known as a table? A hand? When we take the name away — the culturally condoned concept of what a thing is — what remains if not a vibrant, endless mystery of sheer aliveness presenting itself in form? The more we wonder at the immediate world we live in, the closer — the more intimate, inextricably joined — we are likely to feel to this throbbing, wild, and passionate world. The moment I see behind the names of things, I, too, come alive as the world comes alive in its essential, shimmering beauty.

Of course, the gift of language is a marvel in itself. It is what makes us human. We live in a knowledge society, and language is the currency that makes our knowledge-based world possible. But language is also an enchantment that serves to veil what is always before our eyes. We are conditioned today to refer everything to the logic of the rational mind and to Google. Why would we even think of dropping the need to know? The need to know has brought us all the way from stone axes to endovascular surgery in just a few thousand years. Everything we now take for granted — the Internet, space travel, algorithms, Google Earth, the postmodern novel — is built on a vast store of knowledge that has taken millennia to develop. That knowledge is civilization as we know it.

And yet behind our knower's mind is the vast ocean of knowing that doesn't know anything in particular. This is what neuroscientists are looking for under the designation of *consciousness*. The discovery of the nature of consciousness and whether it exists independently of brain functioning is the current holy grail of science. Yet science can never take us beyond the names of things, least of all beyond our own names. Science can only ever tell us *about* things, and only from the stance of an observer looking at the flicker of lights on a computer screen. Science chases whatever can be objectified, set at a distance and apparently separate from the observer.

But who we are can never be objectified, only experienced. Our thoughts, feelings, and sensations can be followed with a brain scanner, but who we are independent of those traces on the computer screen — whoever it is that is aware of those thoughts and feelings — can only be known with a wordless knowing, an occupying, embodying, of the awareness that lives as us. Science will never reveal who you are, what you are here for, where you are going and why. Its realm is the objective, not the inherently subjective, world of being. As for language — including the words you are reading now — it points to the moon without ever knowing the moon.

~

When faced with the great question of our existence, we can only let go of the need to know objectively. When we fall back from identifying with the knowledge we have accumulated over a lifetime, then the dimension of conscious being, which is ever present, becomes apparent in the foreground. We can be who we are, inhabit who we are — a loving, aware presence — without knowing the answer to who we are. In being, there are no questions and no answers. Those belong to the frontal cortex. Being is nonlocatable yet ever present. To rest in being is to be who you are, knowingly.

In the moments of space *between* thoughts — positive or negative — when you are just out for a stroll, sitting in meditation, or lying in a hammock, in those moments between sleeping and waking, in any moment at all, then from out of that space, as if out of nowhere, a deeper knowing can emerge into action; and you just know, you know with every cell of your body, that your life is calling you to follow it where it needs to go. The kind of action that arises from that knowing is not the result of a decision or deliberation. It is a spontaneous upwelling from out of the vast and unending fabric of existence — sheer poetry, utter foolishness, pure wisdom.

And it can only happen now, when I let go of looking over my shoulder or around the next corner and allow what is before me to enter me on its own terms, which are always surprising and more alive than what has just gone before. I can finally live in the vividness of now and know that my blood is running warm rather than with the lost heat of yesterday.

Rumi says,

Sell your cleverness
And buy bewilderment.

(FROM *THE MASNAVI*,
TRANSLATED BY EDWARD WHINFIELD)

In this moment there is only the cawing of crows and the hum of the fridge and everywhere the loving silence that encompasses all things in a seamless intimacy of the one mysterious life that animates everything and everyone, that traces these words across the white page and gives sound and form and color and smell to everything as it inexplicably arises and falls away. There is no longer any knower or known but only one endless field of loving awareness in which there are no questions or answers but simply the tenderness, the sheer beauty of existence, that shimmers and glistens around us now wherever we are.

When we forget what we know, the tenderness of the world, the sheer beauty of it, can rise up to meet us. We can belong again. We can feel the motions of that tenderness, and trust the intimacy of being held always in an embrace that in reality never left us and never will. Then we can trust that not only life, but also death, is perfectly safe.

ACKNOWLEDGMENTS

TRUE GRATITUDE first and foremost to all the teachers and individuals whose presence, love, and wisdom have touched my life and helped shape my way of being and seeing. Gratitude, too, to all those I have stolen words of wisdom from and used for my own purposes in this book. A deep bow to Braeda Horan and Athena Katsaros for allowing me to tell their inspiring stories. And another deep bow is unquestionably due to Jason Gardner, whose editor's insight and eye are second to none. Finally, I am grateful that Kim Corbin, New World Library publicist, was assigned to bring the strong wind of her enthusiasm to fill the book's sail.

NOTES

INTRODUCTION

Page 3, *"There was a lot of skin diving"*: Rick Hanson, "Get Out of the War," *Resources for Happiness, Love, and Wisdom* (newsletter), July 7, 2015, www.rickhanson.net/category/just-one-thing /go-green.

Page 4, *"Out in the Arctic, I was aware"*: Sarah Lewis, *The Rise: Creativity, the Gift of Failure, and the Search for Mastery* (New York: Simon & Schuster, 2015).

Page 6, *Research done by neuroscientist Arne Dietrich*: Ed Slingerland, *Trying Not to Try: Ancient China, Modern Science, and the Power of Spontaneity* (New York: Crown, 2014).

DROPPING THE STRUGGLE FOR A PERFECT LIFE

Page 36, *"One day Ajahn Chah held up a beautiful Chinese teacup."*: Jack Kornfield, *The Wise Heart: A Guide to the Universal Teachings of Buddhist Psychology* (New York: Bantam, 2009).

Page 41, *"Why do you want to shut out of your life"*: Rainer Maria Rilke, *Letters to a Young Poet*, trans. Stephen Mitchell (New York: Vintage, 1986).

Page 44, *"There is this element of just surrendering"*: Barry Magid, interview, at www.wisdompubs.org/blog/201403/everyone -comes-meditation-practice-wrong-reason-conversation -psychoanalyst-barry-magid.

Page 46, *"The one who learns to live"*: Carl Jung, *The Red Book: A Reader's Edition* (New York: Norton, 2012).

Page 47, *Suddenly it was as if the ground*: Carl Jung, *Memories, Dreams, Reflections* (New York: Random House, 1961).

DROPPING THE STRUGGLE FOR MEANING AND PURPOSE

Page 56, *"What if I should be more famous than Gogol"*: Leo Tolstoy, *A Confession and Other Religious Writings*, trans. Jane Kentish (1879; repr., New York: Penguin, 1987).

Page 63, *"If life has a base that it stands upon"*: Virginia Woolf, "A Sketch of the Past," in *Moments of Being*, ed. Jeanne Schulkind (1976; repr., New York: Mariner, 1985).

DROPPING THE STRUGGLE WITH TIME

Page 96, *"Getting stuff done sometimes seems like the secular religion"*:

Rick Hanson, "Drop the Load," *Resources for Happiness, Love, and Wisdom* (newsletter), September 5, 2015, www.rickhanson.net /category/just-one-thing/go-green.

Page 98, *"I only went out for a walk"*: John Muir, *John of the Mountains: The Unpublished Journals of John Muir*, ed. Linnie Marsh Wolfe (1938; repr., Madison: University of Wisconsin Press, 1979).

Page 99, *"Leisure is not the privilege of those"*: This discussion of leisure and the mention of David Steindl-Rast came from www.brain pickings.org.

Dropping the Struggle with Change

Page 109, *"When I enter most intimately"*: David Hume, *A Treatise of Human Nature: Being an Attempt to Introduce the Experimental Method of Reasoning into Moral Subjects* (1739; repr., Wotton-under-Edge, UK: Clarendon Press, 2011).

Page 118, *"Every day Thay continues to remind us"*: "An Update on Thay's Health," the nuns and monks of Plum Village (newsletter), September 8, 2015, Plumvillage.org/news/an-update-on-thays -health-8th-september-2015.

PERMISSIONS ACKNOWLEDGMENTS

ABOUT THE AUTHOR

ROGER HOUSDEN IS THE AUTHOR of twenty-three books, including the best-selling Ten Poems series. All his books explore perennial human questions through the use of poetry, art, or pilgrimage. His work has been featured in the *New York Times*, the *Lost Angeles Times*, and *O: The Oprah Magazine*. He uses writing as a teaching tool for personal exploration and reflection and runs regular courses around the country.

www.rogerhousden.com